S0-ADL-738

BELTANE

Welcome the Season of Fertility, Flowers, and Fairies with a Maypole Dance

The spring season has always been a time of celebration and merriment. The appearance of flowers after a cold winter is a promise of warm summer days to come. Many of the modern celebrations of May are rooted in ancient Pagan traditions that honor the earth and the forces that renew life.

The Maypole is the symbol of the spirit of vegetation returning and renewing its life with the approach of summer. Traditionally, the Maypole was topped with a wreath that symbolized the fertile power of nature. Ribbons, an ancient talisman of protection dating back to archaic Roman religion, were attached to the pole to ensure the safety of the newborn season. Celebrants encircled the Maypole and danced in a symbolic weaving of human life with the life of nature itself.

About the Author

Raven Grimassi is the author of several books on Wicca/Witchcraft including the award-winning *Wiccan Mysteries* (1998 Book of the Year and Best Spirituality Book by the Coalition of Visionary Retailers at the International New Age Trade Show). Grimassi has been a practitioner and teacher of Wicca/Witchcraft for over twenty-five years; former students include authors Scott Cunningham and Donald Michael Kraig. Grimassi is currently directing Elder of the Arician Tradition, and the editor of *Raven's Call*, a journal of modern Wicca/Witchcraft.

Raven Grimassi was trained in the family tradition of Italian Witchcraft and is also an initiate of several other traditions including Brittic Witchcraft and the Pictish-Gaelic tradition. He has appeared on television and radio nationwide in his efforts to educate the public concerning the erroneous stereotypes related to Wicca/Witchcraft. Grimassi is a frequent guest speaker at major festivals and a popular lecturer and presenter of workshops on magick, ritual, and Wicca/Witchcraft.

To Write to the Author

If you wish to contact the author or would like more information about this book, please write to the author in care of Llewellyn Worldwide and we will forward your request. Both the author and publisher appreciate hearing from you and learning of your enjoyment of this book and how it has helped you. Llewellyn Worldwide cannot guarantee that every letter written to the author can be answered, but all will be forwarded. Please write to:

Raven Grimassi
c/o Llewellyn Worldwide
P.O. Box 64383, Dept. 1-56718-283-6
St. Paul, MN 55164-0383, U.S.A.

Please enclose a self-addressed stamped envelope for reply, or $1.00 to cover costs.
If outside U.S.A., enclose international postal reply coupon.

Many of Llewellyn's authors have websites with additional information and resources. For more information, please visit our website at
http://www.llewellyn.com

Springtime Rituals, Lore & Celebration

BELTANE

RAVEN GRIMASSI

2001
Llewellyn Publications
St. Paul, Minnesota 55164-0383, U.S.A.

Beltane: Springtime Rituals, Lore & Celebration © 2001 by Raven Grimassi. All rights reserved. No part of this book may be used or reproduced in any manner whatsoever, including Internet usage, without written permission from Llewellyn Publications except in the case of brief quotations embodied in critical articles and reviews.

FIRST EDITION
First Printing, 2001

Book design and editing by Connie Hill
Cover design and interior illustrations by Anne Marie Garrison
Cover illustration © 2000 by Lauren O'Leary

Library of Congress Cataloging-in-Publication Data
Grimassi, Raven, 1951–
    Beltane : springtime rituals, lore & celebration / Raven Grimassi. — 1st ed.
        p. cm.
    Includes bibliographical references and index.
    ISBN 1-56718-283-6
    1. Beltane. 2. May Day. 3. Witchcraft. I. Title.

BF1572.B4 G75   2001
394.2627—dc21   00-066960

Llewellyn Worldwide does not participate in, endorse, or have any authority or responsibility concerning private business transactions between our authors and the public.

    All mail addressed to the author is forwarded but the publisher cannot, unless specifically instructed by the author, give out an address or phone number.

Any Internet references contained in this work are current at publication time, but the publisher cannot guarantee that a specific location will continue to be maintained. Please refer to the publisher's website for links to authors' websites and other sources.

Llewellyn Publications
A Division of Llewellyn Worldwide, Ltd.
P.O. Box 64383, Dept. 1-56718-283-6
St. Paul, MN 55164-0383, U.S.A.
www.llewellyn.com

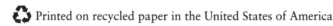 Printed on recycled paper in the United States of America

394.2627
G861b

DEDICATION

To all who continue to light the ancient fires and dance
the ancient dance; the Old Ways will never be forgotten.

APR 1 1 2001
DUERRWAECHTER MEMORIAL LIBRARY
GERMANTOWN, WISCONSIN 53022

Other Books by Raven Grimassi

Wiccan Magick

Wiccan Mysteries

Italian Witchcraft

Hereditary Witchcraft

Encyclopedia of Wicca & Witchcraft

CONTENTS

Recipes for Celebrating May:
• A Quick May Wine • Blessing for May Wine • Making a May Cup
• Bacchus Pudding • Custard • Porridge
• May Wreath Cake • May Serpent Cake • Oat Cakes (Bannocks)

The Fertile Month of May:
• To Increase Chances of Pregnancy • For Morning Sickness
• To Calm a Threatened Miscarriage • Nursing
• Herbal Treatment Related to a Woman's Body
• To Stimulate and Balance Menstrual Flow
• To Ease a Heavy Menstrual Flow • For Painful Periods
• Hormonal Normalizers

CHAPTER SIX
A MAY RITUAL, 123

The Altar:
• Preparation of an Altar • Preparation of the Ritual Circle

Solitary May Celebration Ritual

Group May Celebration Ritual

CHAPTER SEVEN
ARTS AND CRAFTS, 139

May Wreath

May Garland

Maypole Centerpiece

May Day Cone Basket

Pentacle Hair Braids

INTRODUCTION

Deprived of root, and branch and rind,
Yet flowers I bear of every kind:
And such is my prolific power,
They bloom in less than half an hour.

—Jonathan Swift, *A Maypole*

In this book about the celebration of the May season you will discover the meaning of May, its history, and the traditions associated with May. I have also included traditional and modern crafts for creating centerpieces and other decorations. In modern times May is associated with flowers, Mother's Day, and Memorial Day. Centuries prior to the modern observance of May, this month was an even more celebrated one. Great festivals and street processions of the past included the Maypole and a character known as the Green Man. He was also known by the names "Green George" and "Jack-in-the-Green." This character was the symbol of life, fertility, and growth.

The renewal of life in Nature, symbolized by the emergence of flowers in the May season, is a powerful symbol of the earth as a life-giving mother figure. The ancient people believed that the earth itself was a conscious living being, the Great Earth Mother. The ancient figure of the Green Man, the spirit of plant life, might be thought of as the consort of the Earth Mother. His image thrived in festivals and street processions until the late nineteenth century, but by the end of that century he had all but disappeared. If not for images of the Green Man on an occasional pub sign and magazine advertisement, along with brief mentions in folklore writings, we might have completely lost sight of him as we passed into the twentieth century.

By the arrival of the twentieth century, farm work had given way to factory work. Cities continued to expand and engulf the surrounding land. Train tracks and roadways cut across the face of countryside. It was during this stage that the celebrations of May Day and other time-honored festival occasions began to decline. Jobs in the city drew people away from the farms and the country. Because no labor laws existed during this time, people were forced to work long hours, six days a week. Fewer people worked the farmlands and the focus of life turned to materialism. World War I took many young farmers off to battle, many never returned, and the impact of this war took its toll on the European way of life.

The traditions that once empowered and vitalized us withered into quaint customs associated with the less sophisticated. Humankind parted ways with the earth and embraced mechanization and world politics. The only memory of Jack-in-the-Green now is a potted plant in a home or apartment.

Here in the beginning of the twenty-first century we can clearly see the effect our progress as a civilization has had upon Nature and the earth. The atmosphere is polluted with the smoke of our factories and the exhaust of our machines. The most fertile lands lie now beneath asphalt parking lots surrounding shopping malls. Our rivers, lakes, streams, and oceans are contaminated with chemicals and waste materials. For the health of our planet, and the health of our minds, we must dance again with the Green Man and raise up the old Maypole. We must call Jack-in-the-Green back into our lives and remember what is worth celebrating.

In the chapters of this book are suggestions for aligning oneself with Nature again through embracing the images of old May celebrations. In folk magic it is said, "Like attracts like," and we draw to ourselves those things that are reflected in the symbolism with which we surround ourselves. By using the symbols of May presented in this book we can once again embrace the ways of Nature and move closer to living with her in a common cause.

THE CELEBRATION
OF MAY

I sing of brooks, of blossoms, birds, and bowers;
Of April, May, of June, and July-flowers,
I sing of May-poles, Hock-carts, wassails, wakes,
Of bride-grooms, brides, and of their bridal-cakes.

—Robert Herrick

Since ancient times the May season has been a time of celebration and merriment. The appearance of flowers after a cold winter season signals the promise of warm summer days to come. Many of the modern celebrations of May are rooted in ancient pagan traditions that honored the earth and the forces that renewed life. In many pre-Christian European regions, Nature was perceived as a goddess and from this ancient concept evolved the modern "Mother Nature" personification.

May Day celebrations are a time to acknowledge the return of growth and the end of decline within the cycle of life. The rites of May are rooted in ancient fertility festivals that can be traced back to the Great Mother festivals of the Hellenistic period of Greco-Roman religion. The Romans inherited the celebration of May from earlier Latin tribes such as the Sabines. The ancient Roman festival of Floralia is one of the celebrations of this nature. This festival culminated on May 1 with offerings of flowers and garlands to the Roman goddesses Flora and Maia, for whom the month of May is named. Wreaths mounted on a pole, which was adorned with a flowered garland, were carried in street processions in honor of the goddess Maia.

With the expansion of the Roman Empire into Gaul and the British Isles, the festivals of May were introduced into Celtic religion. Various aspects of May celebrations such as the blessing of holy wells are traceable to the ancient Roman festival of Fontinalia, which focused upon offerings to spirits that revived wells and streams. Even the Maypole itself is derived from archaic Roman religion. In the *Dictionary of Faiths & Folklore* by W. C. Hazlitt (London: Bracken Books, 1995), the author states that in ancient Briton it was the custom to erect Maypoles adorned with flowers in honor of the Roman goddess Flora.

The Maypole is traditionally a tall pole garlanded with greenery or flowers and often hung with ribbons that are woven into complex patterns by a group of dancers. Such performances are the echoes of ancient dances around a living tree in spring rites designed to ensure fertility. Tradition varies as to the type of wood used for the maypole. In some accounts the traditional wood is ash or birch, and in others it is cypress or elm. The Maypole concept can be traced to a figure known as a herms (or *hermai*) that was placed at the crossroads throughout the Roman Empire.

A herms is a pillar-like figure sporting the upper torso of a god or spirit. The herms was a symbol of fertility and it was often embellished by an erect penis protruding from the pillar. The earliest herms were simply wooden columns upon which a ritual mask was hung. In time, to reduce replacement costs, the Romans began making the herms from stone instead of wood. In May, the herms was adorned with flowers and greenery, and sacred offerings were placed before it. This and other practices of ancient Italian paganism were carried by the Romans throughout most of continental Europe and into the British Isles. For further information on this topic the reader is referred to *Dionysos: Archetype Image of Indestructible Life* by Carl Kerenyi (Princeton: Princeton University Press, 1976, pp. 380–381).

In 1724 the noted occultist Dr. William Stuckely, in his work titled the *Itinerarium*, describes a Maypole near Horn Castle, Lincolnshire, that reportedly stood on the site of a former Roman herms (a wood or stone carving of the upper torso of a body emerging from a pillar). The author records that boys "annually keep up the festival of the Floralia on May Day," and carried white willow wands covered with cowslips. Stuckely goes on to say that these wands are derived from the thyrsus wands once carried in the ancient Roman Bacchanal rites. For further information on this, I refer the reader to Hazlitt's *Dictionary of Faiths & Folklore* (pp. 402–406).

May festivals commonly incorporate elements of pre-Christian worship related to agricultural themes. In ancient times a young male was chosen to symbolize the spirit of the plant kingdom. Known by such names as Jack-in-the-Green, Green George, and the Green Man, he walked in a procession through the villages symbolizing his return as spring moves toward summer. Typically a pretty young woman bearing the title "Queen of the May" led the procession. She was accompanied by a young man selected as the May King, typically symbolized by Jack-in-the-Green. The woman and man, also known as the May Bride and Bridegroom, carried flowers and other symbols of fertility related to agriculture.

The connection of the tree to May celebrations is quite ancient and is rooted in archaic tree worship throughout Europe. The belief that the gods dwelled within trees was widespread. Later this tenet diminished into a belief that the spirit of vegetation resided in certain types of trees, such as the oak, ash, and hawthorn. In many parts of Europe young people would gather branches and carry them back to their villages on May 1 morning, suspending them in the village square from a tall pole. Bringing newly budding branches into the village was believed to renew life for everyone. Dances were performed around this "Maypole" to ensure that everyone was connected or woven into the renewing forces of Nature.

The garland of flowers, associated with May rituals, is a symbol of the inner connections between all things, symbolic of that which binds and connects. Garlands are typically made from plants and flowers that symbolize the season or event for which the garland is hung as a marker or indicator. In ancient Greek and Roman art many goddesses carry garlands, particularly Flora, a flower goddess associated with May. The Maypole is often decorated with a garland as a symbol of fertility, in anticipation of the coming summer and harvest season.

Among the Celtic people the celebration of May was called Beltane, meaning "bright fire," due to the bonfires associated with the ancient rites of this season. This festival occasion was designed as a celebration of the return of life and fertility to a world that has passed through the winter season. It is the third of the four great Celtic fire festivals of the year: Beltane, Imbolc, Lughnasahd, and Samhain. Beltane was traditionally celebrated at the end of April. Many modern Wicca Traditions celebrate Beltane on May 1 or May Eve. Along with its counterpart of Samhain, Beltane divided the Celtic year into its two primary seasons, winter and summer. Beltane marked the beginning of summer's half and the pastoral growing season.

Continental Celts worshipped a god known as Belenus. The root word "Bel" means bright, whether associated with fire or with a light such as the sun. As noted earlier, the word "Beltane" literally means "bright fire" and refers to bonfires (known as "need-fire") lit during this season. Beltane may or may not be derived from the worship of the Celtic deity Belenus (MacKillop, James. *Dictionary of Celtic Mythology*. New York: Oxford University Press, 1998, p. 35). In ancient times Beltane heralded the approach of summer and the promise of fullness. Herds of cattle were ritually driven between two bonfires as an act of purification and protection. This was believed to ensure their safety and fertility throughout the remainder of the year. The fires celebrated the warmth of the sun, and its power to return life and fruitfulness to the soil. Ashes from the sacred bonfires lit at Beltane were scattered over the fields to ensure fertility. An old Welsh custom was to take some ash home for protection, or to put ashes in one's shoe to guard against misfortune.

Many modern Wiccans/Witches believe that the Beltane festival was held in honor of the god Bel. In some modern traditions he is also known as Beli, Balar, Balor, or Belenus. Authors Janet and Stewart Farrar point out that some people have suggested that Bel is the Brythonic Celt equivalent of the god Cernunnos. (Farrar, Janet & Stewart. *Eight Sabbats for Witches*. London: Robert Hale, 1981, pp. 80–81). In modern Wicca/Witchcraft, Beltane marks the appearance of the Horned One, who is the rebirth of the solar God slain during the Wheel of the Year. He then becomes consort to the Goddess, impregnating Her with his seed, and thereby ensuring his own rebirth once again. In the evolution of god images, he became the Harvest Lord of agrarian society. In this regard the god is associated with the Green Man, a popular image connecting the god to the ever-returning cycle of foliage and flowering.

Southern European traditions, such as those of old Italy, celebrate the ripeness of May by tying ribbons and lemons around flowering branches. Potted trees, anointed male and female, are brought into a plaza and married in a mock ceremony. As with all things Italian, food is in abundance and traditional meals are served. Groups of people join together in street processions led by a young woman who carries a garlanded branch decorated with ribbons, fresh fruits, and lemons.

One very interesting observance of May is held in the mountainous region near Cocullo, just east of Rome. Here the inhabitants gather in a snake festival. The snakes are carried into the plaza in terracotta jugs filled with grain. The snakes are then handled by keepers and carried around their shoulders. Observers are coaxed into holding the snakes and the festival becomes very exciting. The origin of this festival is traceable to the ancient rites of an Italic people known as the Marsi. They worshipped a snake goddess known as Angizia. In time legends arose associating her with Circe, an ancient Greek sorceress. Today the goddess Angizia has been replaced by Saint Domenico, who is said to protect people from poisonous snakes. Saint Domenico was previously associated with a miracle connected to the growth of fava beans. Both snakes and fava beans are intimately connected in Italic paganism to themes of emergence from the Underworld.

The snake was first associated with the month of May as a fertility symbol. To the ancients, the snake penetrated the earth, an act suggestive of sexual intercourse. Because the earth was a fertile region, the snake was believed to possess its inner secrets by disappearing into the depths below. In occult lore the snake represents the inner knowledge of creation and is considered a guardian of the waters of life. Due to their ability to shed their skin, snakes symbolize rebirth and eternal life, one of the reasons why snakes appear on the caduceus symbol worn by medical professionals.

OLD MAY CUSTOMS

In his *Dictionary of Faiths & Folklore*, author W. C. Hazlitt recounts a custom practiced among the ancient Romans where young boys "go out Maying" on April 30 to collect branches for celebrating the first of May. A similar custom is still observed today among the Cornish, who decorate their doorways on the first of May with green boughs of sycamore and hawthorn. In Huntingdonshire, people gather sticks for fuel on May Day, an act perhaps related to the Druidic custom of lighting fires on May Day atop the Crugall (Druid's Mound). In northern England it was long the custom to rise at midnight and gather branches in the neighboring woods, adorning them with nosegays and crowns of flowers. At sunrise the gatherers would return home and decorate their doors and windows. In Ireland it was once the custom to fasten a green bough against the home on the first of May to ensure an abundance of milk in the coming summer. Ancient Druids were said to have herded cattle through an open fire on this day in a belief that such an act would keep the cattle from disease all year.

A curious custom of the past called "May Birching" seems to have evolved from the ancient symbolism of trees. On May Eve, participants called "May Birchers" went about various neighborhoods affixing branches or sprigs to the doors of selected houses. The symbolism of what they left there was meant to indicate their sentiments regarding those who dwelled in the respective homes. To leave gorse (in bloom) meant that the woman of the house had a bad reputation. This may be related to an old saying in Northamptonshire: "When gorse is out of bloom, kissing is out of season." The branch of any nut-bearing tree was a sign of open promiscuity. The flowering branch of a hawthorn was a compliment, indicating that the occupants were well liked in the community. However, any other type of thorn indicated that the inhabitants were scorned. The presence of a rowan meant that the people were well loved. To leave briar was an indication that the people were untrustworthy.

Another May custom connected to the theme of gathering is the collection of dew in the early morning on May 1. Among the ancient Romans the dew was sacred to the goddess Diana, who was also known as "The Dewy One." It was believed that the moon left the morning dew during the night. In Italian Witchcraft dew is collected from several sacred plants and is then used as a type of holy water. This holy dew-water of May is believed to bestow good fortune throughout the year. In some parts of Britain young country girls go out just before sunrise on May Day and collect dew from the plants. The dew is then applied to their faces in the belief that it will keep their complexions beautiful and will remove blemishes.

MAY GARLANDS

The May garland is an emblem of summer and is decorated with bright ribbons, fresh leaves, and every type of flower available at the season. Traditionally the May doll is hung suspended inside the hoop of the garland. Garlands have long been associated with May and their use in May celebrations is traceable to the ancient Roman festival of Flora. In the British Isles, peeled willow wands often sport May garlands. The May staves are often adorned with posies or wreaths of cowslips. At Horncastle in Lincolnshire it was once the custom to carry adorned wands in a procession culminating in their placement on a hill where an ancient Roman temple once stood. The flowers of the foxglove plant are traditionally set in place on the May garland in honor of the fairies. (See pp. 143–144 for directions for constructing a May garland.)

THE MAYPOLE

The Maypole is the symbol of the spirit of vegetation returning and renewing its life with the approach of summer. Traditionally the Maypole was topped with a wreath that symbolized the fertile power of Nature. Ribbons, an ancient talisman of protection dating back to archaic Roman religion, were attached to the pole to ensure the safety of the newborn season. Celebrants encircled the pole and danced in a symbolic weaving of human life with the life of Nature itself.

The Maypole appears to have evolved from archaic Roman religion where it began as an object known as a herms, as noted earlier in this chapter. However, some commentators believe that the Maypole originates from the Phrygian pine tree of Attis carried in the sacred processions related to the temple of Cybele. In ancient Roman religion this was connected with the festival known as Hilaria, a joyful rite of merriment that included dancing around a pole. With the spread of Roman influence into northern Europe these elements of Italic paganism were absorbed into Celtic and Germanic religion.

The traditional Maypole dance is both a circular and a spiral dance. It involves alternation of male and female dancers who move in and out from the center to the outer circumference.

Ribbons of various colors are attached to the top of the pole, draping down to the dancers who hold the opposite end. Some Maypoles are painted yellow and black in a spiral design, while others are red and white like a barber's pole. As the dancers move in a circular pattern, the ribbons are woven along the length of the pole. The addition of ribbons to the Maypole in northern Europe was a later development; earlier in southern Europe the use of ribbons was quite prevalent. In April 1644 an ordinance by the Long Parliament outlawed the setting up of Maypoles throughout England and Wales. The ordinance decreed that May 1 was the Lord's Day, and that Maypoles were a heathen vanity giving way to wickedness.

In parts of Italy today the Maypole is still erected during May celebrations. The pole is greased and topped with a wreath that bears a crown. Competitors try to climb the pole and retrieve the crown. The Church in Italy has made several attempts to end May Day celebrations. The first attempt was to change the goddess Maia into the Virgin Mary, which also served to introduce chastity into a rite that originally featured orgies. In later times the Church tried to replace May Day with the celebration of Saint Joseph, making him the patron of workers and trying to displace May Day with Labor Day. (See pp. 141–142 for directions for constructing a May wreath to top a Maypole.)

THE MAYPOLE DANCE

In the traditional Maypole dance, men and women form an alternating circle around the Maypole. Red and white ribbons hang loosely from the top of the pole. Each person takes a ribbon—the men holding the white and the women the red. Then everyone stands facing the Maypole. On cue the women turn to their right and remain in place. The men then turn facing left and take one step out away from the pole, thereby creating two circles of dancers facing one another. As the music begins the dancers move forward, starting a weaving dance. Each person positions their ribbons to cross over and then under each person they meet next in the dance. The alternation of weaving ribbons over and under continues until the ribbons are too short to allow the dance to continue.

The Maypole, symbol of spring, renewal, and fertility. Dancers weave the ribbons around the pole as they dance.

MAY DOLLS

The May doll still appears in May celebrations, although with less frequency over the past century. The May doll's origin is traceable to the Roman celebrations of the goddess Flora, associated with the month of May. On May 1 images of the May goddess were once carried in ceremonial processions. In many parts of Europe a tradition arose in which the May doll was carried from house to house. The face of the doll was hidden by a piece of lace or a white handkerchief. The householders were asked if they would like to see the May doll, the May lady, or the queen of May. If

they replied yes, they were expected to pay for the privilege, and only after a gift had been made to the bearers was the covering removed and the luck-bringing face displayed to viewers. Young girls went about the village in pairs or in groups of three, carrying a garland with a veiled doll in the center, and singing verses of the traditional May song of their district. Like so many of the old customs and traditions, this one has also disappeared over the years.

The May doll, traditionally carried from door to door to bestow good luck on householders.

THE BELTANE FIRE

In ancient times it was reportedly the Celtic custom to light bonfires on the first of May. In the central Highlands of Scotland such fires were known as the Beltane fires. According to James Frazer, in his book *The Golden Bough* (New York: Macmillan, 1922), traces of human sacrifices have been found to be associated with the Celtic celebration of Beltane. The custom of lighting the bonfires appears to have continued well into the eighteenth century in various regions of Europe. Frazer states that vestiges of ancient Beltane celebrations (originating from Druidic practices) were observed in some parts of the Highlands even as late as his own era, circa 1896.

The Beltane festival included feasting and lighting bonfires on hills or eminences. On May Eve all the fires in the country were extinguished. The people of each hamlet arose on May morning and prepared the materials for igniting the sacred fire of the new Beltane.

The people dug out a trench and placed a pile of wood in the middle, which they kindled with need-fire. One of the oldest traditions involved using a well-seasoned plank of oak with a hole bored in the center. A wimble,* also made of oak, was then fitted to the hole and furiously manipulated to cause heat friction. As soon as sparks appeared handfuls of agaric gathered from old birch trees were tossed in. This material is reportedly extremely combustible and the fire burst forth as though by magic. Frazer states that the sudden burst of flames gave the appearance of having fallen from heaven and that because of this many magical virtues were ascribed to the fire. According to old lore the Beltane fire prevented or cured malignant diseases, particularly in cattle. It was also said to neutralize any poisons.

Once the fire was ablaze the celebrants prepared the feast, ate, and joined together in singing and dancing around the fire. Near the close of the ceremony the facilitator brought out the Beltane cake, a large cake baked with eggs and scalloped around the edge. It was then divided into a

---

* The wimble is a hand tool used for boring or drilling holes.

number of pieces and distributed to those assembled at the celebration. One of the slices bore a mark—the person who received it was then called *cailleach beal-tine*, the Beltane carline. This title brought the person a great deal of chiding, and following the bestowment of this title, several of the celebrants captured him and pretended to toss him in the fire. Then other celebrants would come to his aid and rescue him from entering into the fire. According to Frazer the victim was sometimes thrown to the ground and pelted with eggshells. For the duration of the feast he was then regarded as though dead. The unfortunate individual then retained the loathsome title of cailleach beal-tine for the rest of the year. This custom is quite likely derived from the earlier Druidic human sacrifices that took place at the time of Beltane.

In *The Golden Bough*, Frazer gives the account of a man named Thomas Pennant, who traveled in Perthshire in the year 1769. Pennant recorded:

> On the first of May, the herdsmen of every village hold their Bel-tien, a rural sacrifice. They cut a square trench on the ground, leaving the turf in the middle; on that they make a fire of wood, on which they dress a large caudle of eggs, butter, oatmeal and milk; and bring besides the ingredients of the caudle, plenty of beer and whisky; for each of the company must contribute something. The rites begin with spilling some of the caudle on the ground, by way of libation: on that every one takes a cake of oatmeal, upon which are raised nine square knobs, each dedicated to some particular being, the supposed preserver of their flocks and herds, or to some particular animal, the real destroyer of them: each person then turns his face to the fire, breaks off a knob, and flinging it over his shoulders, says, "This I give to thee, preserve thou my horses; this to thee, preserve thou my sheep; and so on." After that, they use the same ceremony to the noxious animals:

"This I give to thee, O fox! spare thou my lambs; this to thee, O hooded crow! this to thee, O eagle!" When the ceremony is over, they dine on the caudle; and after the feast is finished, what is left is hid by two persons deputed for that purpose; but on the next Sunday they reassemble, and finish the reliques of the first entertainment.

Oat cakes, sometimes called the Beltane bannock, are associated with Beltane and still appear in May Day celebrations in some parts of the British Isles. According to Frazer there was also a cheese made on the first of May, which was kept until the next Beltane as a charm to ward off any bewitching of milk products. Similar Beltane customs appear throughout the British Isles. In Wales the custom of lighting Beltane fires varied and took place anywhere from the eve of May Day to the third day of May. Frazer described the Welsh tradition in this manner:

Nine men would turn their pockets inside out, and see that every piece of money and all metals were off their persons. Then the men went into the nearest woods, and collected sticks of nine different kinds of trees. These were carried to the spot where the fire had to be built.

There a circle was cut in the sod, and the sticks were set crosswise. All around the circle the people stood and watched the proceedings. One of the men would then take two bits of oak, and rub them together until a flame was kindled. This was applied to the sticks, and soon a large fire was made. Sometimes two fires were set up side by side. These fires, whether one or two, were called coelcerth or bonfire. Round cakes of oatmeal and brown meal were split in four, and placed in a small flour-bag, and everybody present had to pick out a portion. The last bit in the bag fell to the lot of the bag-holder. Each person who chanced to pick up a piece of brown-meal cake was compelled to leap three times over the flames, or to run thrice between the two fires, by which means the people thought they were sure of a plentiful harvest. Shouts and screams of those who had to face the ordeal could be heard ever so far, and those who chanced to pick the oatmeal portions sang and danced and clapped their hands in approval, as the holders of the brown bits leaped three times over the flames, or ran three times between the two fires.

The folk belief held that by leaping thrice over the bonfires, or running thrice between them, a plentiful harvest was ensured. In the Welsh tradition the bonfires protected the land from evil forces so that the crops would grow and thrive without interference. The heat of the fires was thought to fertilise the fields by quickening the seeds in the ground. The ashes were considered to possess power imparted from the fire and were carried in small charm bags.

The Beltane fires appear to have been kindled also in Ireland where the Druids oversaw the driving of cattle between the bonfires as a safeguard against disease.

The custom of driving cattle through or between fires on May Day or the eve of May Day persisted in Ireland for many centuries after the decline of the Druids.

The first historical references to Beltane fires come from the writings of Julius Caesar in his military campaign against the Celts. The Beltane tradition of lighting bonfires involved a specific ritual. From a hill overlooking the village the men prepared by first cutting the turf away in a circle or square, leaving a block of turf in place in the center. Within this clearing they laid the wood in a cross-hatched pattern. By custom the wood bundle was decorated with wool ribbons and hawthorn flowers.

Beltane fires represent healing and other virtues. The heat of the fires was thought to encourage seeds to sprout.

At a given point, all the hearth fires of the village were extinguished and the people gathered at the hill. With them they carried the ingredients for a communal feast. This included milk, butter, eggs, oats, oatcakes, and a good supply of ale or mead. The first fire of the season was called "need-fire" (*tein-eigin*). It was ignited by the old method of wood friction or flint stone sparks. Fires lighted afterward were called bonfires (*coelcerth*) or bale-fires. Traditionally livestock were driven between the fire pits three times around the flames deosil. This was done to bring good fortune, protection, and fertility.

After the bonfire was kindled, the villagers prepared and shared a feast of eggs, milk, oats and butter, with bannock or oat cakes. Once the ritual festivities ended, the ashes from the Beltane fires were spread from field to field in a belief that they made the land fertile. As noted earlier some commentators feel that human and/or animal sacrifice was practiced in the early periods of Beltane ritual by the Celts. The spreading of ashes in the field may support this idea since in many ancient cultures the cremated ashes of kings and hero figures were often spread in such a manner.

THE SPIRITS
OF MAY

*The month of May was come, when every lusty
heart beginneth to blossom, and to bring forth fruit;
for like as herbs and trees bring forth fruit and
flourish in May, in likewise every lusty heart that is
in any manner a lover, springeth and flourisheth in
lusty deeds.*

—Sir Thomas Malory

In ancient times our ancestors worshipped trees as deities. Following this concept came the veneration of trees as powerful spirits. In time the tree came to be viewed, not as the deity or spirit itself, but as the dwelling place of such an entity. This was an important stage of development as animism (the attribution of conscious life to natural objects) passed over into polytheism. In primitive magical reasoning, once an entity was separated from the trees it became instead a forest deity. Eventually forest deities were given human shape and characteristics. From this formula arose many pagan spirits and deities associated with plant life and woodland areas.

The May season is associated with a number of curious figures that have their origins in pre-Christian religion. Some of the best known are Jack-in-the-Green, Green George, the Wild Man, and the Green Man. The figure of Green George exists in one form or another all over Europe. In England, the Green George figure is covered with shrubbery to the point that only his eyes are visible. In May processions Green George is carried in a wicker cage from which he peers out at the gathered spectators. In pre-Christian times Green George was the "bringer of summer," and he who heralds the rising waxing forces of Nature. To many, Green George is the personification of summer itself.

The character known as Jack-in-the-Green was once the principal figure featured in May celebrations. In England he had a curious connection to the society of chimney sweeps until the end of the nineteenth century when many of the old street celebrations began to disappear. When we consider that wood is burned in the fireplace and that Jack-in-the-Green is a spirit of the greenwood, the chimney sweeps may have symbolized the caretakers of the sacred fire-pit that renewed the spirit of vegetation. It had long been the custom in Europe to burn effigies associated with the changing of the year. This burning sacrifice was intended to drive out the old and bring in the new, the theme of decline and renewal in the cycle of Nature. In Italy this was still observed as late as the mid-twentieth century, during the festival of Befana.

THE MAY QUEEN AND KING

In pre-Christian European religion the spirit of vegetation is often known as the King or Queen of the Woodlands. The association of the May Queen with May Day is a long-standing tradition. The May Queen presides over the festivities, along with her consort, the May King. She is selected by her peers and is a young maiden, often not older than thirteen. Traditionally the May Queen is the prettiest of the contestants. She is always crowned by her predecessor of the year before.

In the May Day procession the King and Queen of May follow behind the May garland. They are accompanied by four young males who each bear a staff decorated like the Maypole. The figure of the May Queen is traceable to the worship of the Roman goddess Flora whose rites were celebrated on May 1.

On the Isle of Man, as late as the eighteenth century, May Day was marked by a battle between the Queen of May and the Queen of Winter. The Queen of Winter was a man dressed like a woman. Each Queen had a company of followers commanded by a captain. The followers of May were dressed in summer clothes and the followers of winter were in writing garb accordingly. On May morning the two companies met in a mock battle. If the May Queen was captured, she was then ransomed for the cost of the festival arrangements.

DUERRWAECHTER MEMORIAL LIBRARY
GERMANTOWN, WISCONSIN 53022

In other regions of the British Isles the contest between summer and winter is acted out each year at May Day by a troop of boys and a troop of girls. The boys rush from house to house, singing, shouting, and ringing bells to drive winter away. Following the boys come a group of girls, singing softly and led by a May bride, all in bright dresses and bedecked with flowers and garlands to represent the genial advent of spring. Formerly the part of winter was played by a straw man, which the boys carried with them.

The Queen of the May, and the May King,
symbols of the goddess and god of nature.

THE GREEN MAN

The Green Man is the primal consciousness of the plant kingdom. He is one of the oldest spiritual concepts held by humankind. Early humans believed that inanimate objects were spirits or deities. In contrast to this belief, at a certain human stage of development, people believed that inanimate objects were simply the dwelling places of spirits or deities within the material world. In either case the Green Man represents the animation of Nature by an unseen power. The classic image of the Green Man is a human-like face mask covered in leaves.

During the early period, when our ancestors were hunter-gatherers, the forest was a realm beyond comprehension. It was filled with dangerous predators, poisonous snakes, and spiders. The forest also, however, provided shelter and food. The spirit of such a place was an undefined and mysterious character hidden in the plants and trees. When humans became an agricultural society the concept of the plant spirit began to transform. Human reasoning during this stage concluded that because plants were grown from seeds, the spirit of the Green Man must be within the seed. Ancient people viewed the plant that issued forth from the seed as a manifestation of the spirit that once dwelled within the seed. When the time came to harvest the plant, the spirit was believed to flee from bundle to bundle as the harvest was stacked in the fields. Therefore it was vital to capture the fleeing spirit inside the last harvested bundle before it could totally escape the field. Once bound in such a manner, the Green Man spirit could be returned to the soil where he would make the seeds even more powerful for the spring season.

An interesting folk custom related to the harvest season arose in many European communities. When a stranger appeared in the community he was viewed as the plant spirit trying to sneak off unnoticed in the guise of a human. There are still cases in which a visitor to a farm community during the time of harvest is captured and harassed by the locals. Often this person is tied up and held for a short time—according to the locals this is all done in good sport. When no strangers appear at harvest time the last reaper in the field symbolically becomes the plant spirit and is subject to the same treatment. In folk belief the plant spirit, driven out by the cutting of the last sheaf, must now take on another form. Therefore he passes into the reaper who becomes the embodiment of the spirit. In folklore the spirit

The Green Man, symbol of the ever-renewing cycle of life.

of the plant has been personified in such folk characters as Jack-in-the-Green and John Barleycorn.

With the rise of Christianity, the attention given to the Green Man began to diminish. However, a careful examination of the pillars inside many old churches and cathedrals in Europe will reveal Green Man faces hidden within the ornamentation. On occasion the leaves appear to grow out of the mouth and cover a humanoid face. Sometimes the sole configuration of the leaves forms a human-like face. Some of the earliest examples appeared in churches and cathedrals around the sixth century. Reportedly, Bishop Nicetius of Trier ordered the removal of Green Man carvings from the ruin of a nearby Roman temple and had them incorporated into a pair of pillars in the cathedral at Trier. These Green Man images were eventually obscured during restoration work in the eleventh century.

JACK-IN-THE-GREEN

The figure of Jack-in-the-Green is a comparatively modern image when measured against the Green Man character. However, there are references to him as early as 1583 in the journals of Sir Humphrey Gilbert. Jack-in-the-Green is a more defined and clearer personification of the plant spirit than is the Green Man image. His most common image depicts a multi-foliate head peering out through hedges or bushes. Jack-in-the-Green is sometimes called the Hidden One who guards the greenwood. In *The Golden Bough* by Sir James Frazer the author associates Jack-in-the-Green with the celebration of the life-force, and links him with the typical leaf-clad mummer found throughout Europe. Frazer also states that the Jack-in-the-Green is the living May tree and that the May doll figure is an extension of the Jack-in-the-Green character.

The Jack-in-the-Green figure was featured in May Day revels as late as the nineteenth century. At this period he was associated with the chimney sweeps who attended the May festival dressed in gaudy tinsel and ribbons,

Jack-in-the-Green, the primal spirit of forests
and fields in their natural state.

with blackened faces. In a manner not unlike the morris dancers, they danced around a Jack-in-the-Green figure to the music of drums, sticks, shovels, and whistles. The Jack-in-the-Green figure around which they danced was a framework of wicker covered with leaves. Inside was a man peering out from a small gap left in structure. Tradition required that the wicker Jack-in-the-Green had to be built by the chimney sweeps themselves.

Some commentators have suggested that the folk hero Robin Hood may be, in part, an evolution of the Jack-in-the-Green character. One of the oldest folk names for Robin Hood is Robin o' the Hood (Robin of the Hood). Some people have seen in this name the image of a man covered (hooded) in the green of the forest. A once popular British television series featured Robin Hood as a priest of the god Herne. Along with his followers, Robin hid in the depths of Sherwood Forest, keeping alive the ancient pagan cult of Herne. It has also been suggested that the figure of Robin Hood was grafted onto an older concept. This concept is that of the King of the Woods, and in the case of Robin Hood, we can see a blending of the Lord of Misrule as well. In such a scenario, Maid Marion becomes the May Queen wed to the Green Man, and the Merry Men become the May Dancers, armed with swords like the morris dancers.

DUSIO, THE TRICKSTER

One of the most primitive and curious forms of the plant spirit is found in the Etruscan character known as Dusio. In Etruscan art he is depicted very much like the Green Man images later found in other parts of Europe. Following the decline of the Etruscan Empire, Dusio diminished in nature, becoming a sylvan spirit and a follower of Silvanus, the Roman woodland god. Folklorist Charles Leland encountered Dusio as a spirit that inspired "wanton" behavior in men and women, and he equated Dusio with the French spirits known as *Dusii*.

In *Etruscan Roman Remains* (London: T. Fischer Unwin, 1892), Charles Leland speaks of ancient writers such as Livy who spoke of forest demons known as *Drusius*, which Saint Augustine called "ancient spirits" known as *Druten*. Leland suggests that the word "Druten" may be related to the word "Druid." He goes on to say that evidence exists to indicate that the fairy sprite called Robin Goodfellow was of Etruscan origin. In any case, Dusio is clearly a woodland spirit and Leland states that in northern Italy the maiden half fears and half hopes to encounter a handsome elven lover in the deep forest shade. In chapter 9 of *Etruscan Roman Remains*, Leland links Dusio to the spirit of the fireplace. In Italian lore, spirits of fire and the hearth frequently seduce maidservants.

JOHN BARLEYCORN

As noted earlier, the Green Man appears in various forms including Jack-in-the-Green, the character who dances ahead of the May Queen in many May Day processions such as those at Hastings and Knutsford. The Green Man also has his counterpart in one of the oldest Scottish and English folk images, the corn or barley god whose beginnings are rooted in the camps of primitive Neolithic farmers. An old Scottish folk song collected in the early years tells of such a god. He is called John Barleycorn, a mythical figure cut down by three men seeking to prove their prowess. Some commentators feel that, like the Green man, the image of John Barleycorn may represent the God of the Woods, the life spirit, and the spirit of death and resurrection.

The traditional ballad of John Barleycorn reveals several key elements of the nature of the plant spirit:

> *There were three men come out of the west*
> *Their victory to try*
> *And those three men took a solemn vow*

John Barleycorn must die
They plowed, they sowed, they harrowed him in
Throwed clods upon his head
And those three men made a solemn vow
John Barleycorn was dead

They let him lie for a very long time
'Til the rains from heaven did fall
And little Sir John sprung up his head
And so amazed them all,
They let him stand til the midsummer's day
'Til he looked both pale and wan
And Little Sir John's grown a long, long beard
And so became a man.

They hired men with the scythes so sharp to cut
   him off at the knee
They rolled him and tied him around the waist and
   served him barbarously
They hired men with the hard pitchfork
To pierce him through the heart
And the loader he has served him worse than that
For he bound him to a cart

They wheeled him round and around the field 'til
   they came unto a barn
And these three men made a solemn oath on poor
   John Barleycorn
They hired men with the holly club

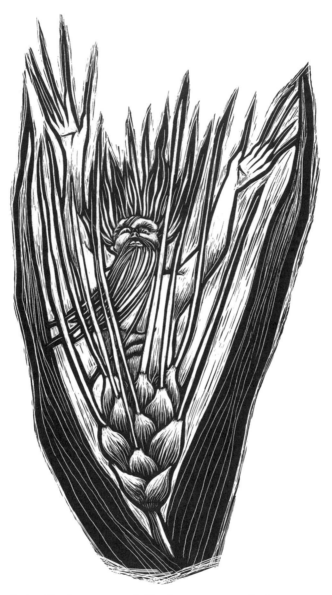

*John Barleycorn: a folk character symbolizing the
spirit of plant life that is always renewed.*

To flay him skin from bone
And the miller he served him worse than that
For he ground him between two stones

Here's Little Sir John in a nut brown bowl
And brandy in the glass
And Little Sir John in the nut brown bowl
Proved the stronger man at last
For the huntsman he can't hunt the fox
Nor so loudly blow his horn
And the tinker he can't mend kettle nor pot
Without a little of the Barleycorn.

The ballad of John Barleycorn describes the planting of the seed or bulb in spring, the growth of the plant at the summer solstice, and the harvesting in the fall season. The ballad speaks of the tenacity of life and the ever-returning cycle within Nature. It tells us that, no matter how much humankind tries to master Nature, Nature will always prevail in the end.

THE HOBBYHORSE

The hobbyhorse is a figure that appears in May Day festivities and is doubtless of pagan origin. The hobbyhorse rides out to greet summer, and it is interesting to note that in ancient Celtic religion May marked the beginning of this season. The hobbyhorse character is a man dressed in a stylized horse costume. The costume consists of a large hoop about six feet round and covered with black material stretched across it. At the front of the hoop is a wooden horse's head with snapper jaws. Traditionally the body of the man in the center of the hoop is covered with a large mask in order to disguise him. However, sometimes the figure of the man appears to be sitting on the horse, as is the case with the morris dancers.

Traditionally the May celebration begins with the hobbyhorse emerging from a tavern. He then parades through town accompanied by a character known as the Teaser or Club Man. The Teaser hops and skips alongside the hobby horse, waving a wand. Eventually the hobbyhorse sinks to the ground as though exhausted. The teaser strokes the horse and brings him back to his feet. From time to time the hobbyhorse character raises his skirt and captures a young maiden beneath it. When she reappears she is wearing a blackened face, and the spectators cheer. It is said that the black mark is for good fortune, and the girl will marry if she is single, or will have a baby within a year if she is married.

Hobbyhorse: a popular character of obscure pagan origins, it is seen used by mummers and swordsmen in street processions. The wooden horse head is attached to a frame and covered with fabric. The rider stands inside the frame and walks the "horse" around.

The hobbyhorse also appears in the May horn dance. He is accompanied by six dancers carrying stag horns and six others carrying swords. Some commentators believe that the hobbyhorse figure is descended from the King of May character, now reduced to the Fool or Buffoon character. As with many of the old traditions, Christian elements have replaced or modified the earlier pagan elements.

MUMMERY, AN ANCIENT TRADITION

Mummery is an old practice that has its roots in primitive magick. Its footprints can be traced back through the mazes of history that lead from England to Germany, to ancient France, and back to pagan Rome and Greece, from where it spread throughout Europe. The early tradition of the Mummers' Play appears in ancient Greece, where groups of strolling players would call at private houses and perform a short play in exchange for food and drink. Such plays depicted a mythical or historical tale, or a story of romance and seduction. The visit of these street performers was thought to bring good luck to the household and the blessings of the gods whose tales were told.

Greek influences flavored the ancient Roman festival of Saturnalia (featuring the agricultural god Saturn), which was marked by unrestrained merry-making. From here mummery evolved and influenced customs that in turn created interesting traditions. As early as 400 B.C., Romans observed the feast of the Saturnalia. They visited family and friends, exchanging gifts and good wishes. The role of master and slave was reversed during this time. Slaves put on the rich robes belonging to their masters, who themselves dressed in wild costumes, roaming the streets with their former slaves. Music filled the streets and there were a multitude of songs and ballads appropriate to the occasion. Social status and the privileges of age and rank were forgotten during the Saturnalia, and everyone was free to give way to personal abandon.

When the Romans became firmly entrenched in ancient Briton, the local inhabitants were practicing a religion based upon a view of the year as divided into winter and summer. Their celebrations were not unlike those of the Saturnalia, and involved much merriment and the consumption of the ale and mead, combined with various forms of sacrifice to their deities. The Romans added Briton to the Roman Empire and held it for over 400 years. The influence of Roman culture and religion had a tremendous impact on all facets of Celtic life.

With the rise of Christianity following the collapse of the Roman Empire, the Church became active in trying to draw the pagans away from their Paganism. Some commentators feel that the Mummers' Play provided a substitute for the pagan sacrifice in the form of symbolic killings that were always part of the mummer's antics. The killings occurred during ritual battles of "good against evil," and were followed by a rebirth of the fallen character. In most plays it was Saint George pitted against the evil Turkish knight. The knight is slain in combat and is then cured by the "doctor" character. The knight then rises and repents of his evil ways, an act that some say symbolizes the death of the Old Year and the birth of the New Year. The mummers also engaged in wild antics during the festivals and encouraged the same of others. Today the mummer is more closely related to the clown, and many modern commentators question the pagan origins of mummery.

3

FAIRY LORE

Child of the pure, unclouded brow
And dreaming eyes of wonder!
Though time be fleet and I and thou
Are half a life asunder,
Thy loving smile will surely hail
The love-gift of a fairy tale.

—Lewis Carroll

35

The month of May, perhaps second only to the revels of midsummer's eve, has long been associated with the gatherings of fairies. The appearance of flowers that herald the approach of summer are signs that the fairy folk are at work in the unveiling of Nature. When people think of fairies today, many often picture beautiful little winged creatures with fragile human features. However the earliest accounts of fairies depict them as dangerous beings that had to be carefully dealt with. Some commentators link fairies to a mythical race of beings known as the Tuatha de Dannan. The Tuatha de Dannan, although portrayed in Celtic legend as mighty heroes, possess certain qualities that have led many commentators to conclude that these figures were once held as gods by the ancient Celts. In the pseudo-history of the Lebor Gabala (Book of Invasions) the Tuatha are defeated by another race called the Milesians and are driven underground. In Celtic legends the realm of the fairy kingdom was accessible through caverns and wells, a theme that eventually led to the identification of the Tuatha de Dannan with the fairy folk.

HISTORICAL AND MYTHICAL BACKGROUND

In many of the old European legends, fairies were visible to humans but kept mostly to themselves. They were able to change their appearance as though their bodies were more fluid than solid in nature. In many tales the fairy could appear as a deer, swan, or a falcon among several other animal forms. In most early legends the transformed fairy creature was milky white with red eyes, a sure sign of it being a fairy in disguise. Later in time, a fairy often appeared as a beautiful woman, detectable only by her graceful air-like movements and a scent of apple blossoms about her.

In many regions of Europe fairy society was divided into two classes, the peasant and the aristocracy. In Wales and Ireland, however, no such division is readily apparent. In Wales fairies were known as *Tylwyth Teg* (the fair family) and in Ireland as *Daoine Side* (mound dwellers). Fairies of the peasant class were generally solitary creatures that served as guardians of fields and forests. The fairies of noble lineage typically belonged to fairy groups and were more powerful beings. In Scandinavia fairy or elven groups were divided into beings of Light and of Darkness. The Light Elves lived in the air and Dark Elves lived underground.

As humans spread further across the land, felling trees and plowing up fields, the fairy race withdrew further into the wilderness. In time, according to legend, they eventually went underground or slipped into the Otherworld. According to old tales, the veil between the worlds was very thin in ancient times, but due to the assault upon Nature by humankind the portal grew thicker. Into the Otherworld disappeared the so-called mythological creatures, returning from time to time, but less so as the centuries passed. By the end of the Middle Ages there are few tales told of actual encounters, and the fairy became an imaginary creature.

The earliest depictions of the familiar fairy image appear in Etruscan tomb art as early as 600 B.C. This is a link that may indicate a connection to the earlier Neolithic Cult of the Dead. The people of this era constructed burial mounds for their dead. Each mound contained a small hole designed to allow the spirit to come and go of its own accord. Over time the belief arose that these spirits went to dwell in the fields and forests, a type of Nature spirit. The Etruscans associated ancestral spirits with beings known as *Lasa*. The Lasa were a fairy-like race. They were winged beings possessing magical powers, and were connected with the Underworld. When the Romans assimilated Etruscan religion, the Lasa spirits became known as *Lare*. In Roman religion the Lare shrines were placed in the home and offerings were made to ancestral spirits. Etruscan art depicts small winged Lasa that are almost always pictured with humans and typically hover over a container of incense or an offering bowl. In archaic Roman religion, the Lare were originally spirits of the land. Shrines and altars were once placed in their honor at the crossroads. Later in Roman religion the Lare also became spirits of demarcation associated with agricultural land.

Images of fairies in Celtic art do not appear until well after the rise of Christianity, following the Roman occupation. In *The Fairy Faith in Celtic Countries* (New York: Citadel Press, 1954), by W. Y. Evans-Wentz (who received his doctorate in folklore from Oxford University), we read that the words *fatua, fata* (Greek and Roman for fairy), and the word *fee* (English for fairy) are all the same word. In chapter 3 the author writes: ". . . the race of immortal damsels whom the old natives of Italy called Fatuae gave origin to all the family of fees . . ." In *The Fairies in English Tradition and Literature* (London: Routledge & Kegan Paul, 1967) by K. M. Briggs (president of the English Folklore Society, doctorate on folklore from Oxford University), the author tells us that the earliest mention of fairies of any kind in England occurred in the Anglo-Saxon charms against elf-shot (from the "Anglo-Saxon Chronicles," circa A.D. 800). In chapter 20 of her book Briggs acknowledges that Celtic belief in fairies may have been derived from Roman mythology and not from classical literature.

In the Etruscan mythos, Lasa spirits are associated with vegetation and the secrets of Nature. In art they are depicted nude and winged, carrying a small vial of elixir. The liquid contained within the vials could produce any of three results. One drop could heal any malady, two drops opened the eyes to the secrets of Nature, and three drops transformed matter into spirit or spirit into matter. Such transformations were necessary in order for anyone to pass between the fairy world and the physical world. Similar concepts also appear later in Celtic fairy legends. Although the beliefs concerning fairies do differ from culture to culture, there are two basic concepts universal in all fairy beliefs: the distortion of time itself, and the hidden entrances to the fairy world. These themes are more prominent in

Celtic mythology. The "trooping" of fairies appears in many Celtic legends and also in the Fairy Cult of Sicily. It does not, however, appear to have been an Etruscan mythos in general. The trooping of fairies is quite common in Italian folklore today.

In *Early Modern European Witchcraft*, edited by Bengt Ankarloo and Gustav Henningsen (Oxford: Clarendon Press, 1993), we find a chapter

In Italy fairies are helpful spirits called Lasa.

devoted to the medieval Fairy Cult in Sicily. The chapter describes this cult as being comprised of an odd number of individuals headed by a queen. She bears such titles as *La Matrona* (the Mother), *La Maestra* (the Teacher), and *Dona Zabella* (The Wise Sybil). Sicilian fairies formed groups called companies, such as the Company of Nobles and the Company of Poor. These fairies had the power to bless fields, cure illnesses, and bestow good fortune. However, if ill-treated they were also capable of causing harm. Only after offerings were made to appease the fairies would they release the offender from their enchantment. Both humans and fairies belonged to companies that were essentially matriarchal (although some males were included). Only the human women could free an offender from a fairy spell, and they were highly revered among the peasant peoples.

Common to fairies of all regions is the belief in the distortion of time. A night spent in a fairy realm often translated into several years in mortal time. Secret entrances always guarded access to these realms and were often found in mounds or tree trunks. Fairies were believed to have a strong aversion to iron, and this metal was used as a protection against them when the need arose. Some folklorists feel that humans who used iron to plow fields and fell trees relate this legend to the use of iron. To the fairies this assault upon Nature was an abomination, and thus the hatred of iron by the fairies. Other folklorists have pointed to legends in which iron traditionally negates the power of magic, acting somewhat like a grounder. One legend tells us that when entering a fairy realm, the person should stick a piece of iron in the door to prevent it from closing. The fairies will not touch the iron, and thus cannot prevent the person from leaving at their will.

As mentioned earlier, fairies were originally considered to be souls of the departed. It wasn't until much later in the Cult of the Dead that they became associated with the elemental kingdoms of Nature. It was believed that the souls of the dead could enter into a living human and possess him or her. Out of this concept arose the tale of fairy changelings left in the crib of human parents. The belief in the *sidhe* or fairies as the dead waiting to return to mortal life may have been a feature of Druidic belief. This probable speculation is supported by early Irish and later Welsh literature. We know from ancient Greek and Roman historians that the Druids were well respected for their knowledge in such areas. In fact, the Mediterranean historians of the time stated that the Druids possessed such a high degree of occult knowledge that they were surpassed only by the Etruscans. The Druids guided the Celts in these matters and maintained a mutually beneficial relationship with the fairy kingdom.

We find in later folklore a great many tales reminding us to always acknowledge the good deeds performed by fairies. It was believed that fairies could both help and harm human beings. Therefore it was always important to thank them for the good fortune they bestowed upon humankind. Out of this mentality arose the practice of saying "knock on wood" when speaking of one's good fortune. This was an acknowledgement that the woodland fairies were being kind. If a person failed to do so, then it could result in the fairies withdrawing their aid, the results of which could be disastrous.

As human society grew from living in simple huts, to villages, and then to towns and cities, rapport with the fairy race began to fade away. Folktales begin to change from frequent encounters with fairies to tales in which various techniques had to be employed to simply allow a person to see a fairy. One such formula was recorded by Hilderic Friend in 1884, citing an unnamed text he claims was written in the year 1600:

> To see fairies put—"A pint of sallet-oyle, and put it into a vial-glasse; but first wash it with rose water and mary-goyle water; the flowers to be gathered towards the East. Wash it till the oyle becomes white; then put it into the glasses, and then put thereto the budds of hollyhocke, the flowers of marygolde, the flowers or toppess of wild thime, the budds of young hazle, and the thime must be

gathered neare the side of a hill where fayries use to be; and take the grasse of a fayrie throne; then all these put into the oyle into the glasse; and sette it to dissolve three dayes in the sunne, and then keep it for thy use."

—*Flowers and Flower Lore*
Reverend Hilderic Friend

THE FAIRY REALM

The kingdoms of the fairy world have been known by many names, such as Tir nan Og, Ynis Gwydrin, and Tim Aill. In them the sun and moon were said to shimmer brighter than in the mortal world. The flowers were more brilliant and all colors within the fairy realm were of greater intensity. In some European tales the fairy kingdom lies on an island and in other tales it is in a cloud or inside the earth. In the tale of "Thomas the Rhymer," the fairy land lies beyond a sea of blood, across an inky heath, and just beyond a bright meadow. From the meadow a gentle path twists along through moss and fern leading into fairyland.

In ancient times lakes, wells, bogs, and all openings in the ground or in trees were considered sacred passages into the Otherworld. Many such sites were marked as sacred by erecting standing stones or stone enclosures at their location. In early fairy lore, to enter the fairy realm was a dangerous venture. One warning that remains consistent in fairy lore is the eating of food while visiting a fairy kingdom. To do so meant that one would be bound to the realm, either for a certain period of time or forever. This theme is quite similar to the legend of Persephone who eats several pomegranate seeds in the Underworld, an act that binds her to return for six months each year. There is a long-standing tradition of offering food to both fairies and the spirits of the dead. The belief underlying this practice held that the spiritual essence was extracted from the food, and it was bad luck for any living thing to eat food previously left for fairies or spirits of the dead.

From the practice of leaving food offerings arose rituals associated with the season of Samhain or All Hallow's/Hallowmas. Here we find food offerings set out for a feast to honor the spirits of the dead, a practice found in the Cult of the Dead that still exists today in Sicily and the British Isles. To partake of offered food is to enter into a relationship with those who offer it. This is one of the most ancient aspects of human culture and is still in use today. To invite someone to have dinner with us, or to be invited, has less to do with eating than it does with relationships. Traditionally the fairy realm is ruled over by a king and queen. Humans who claim to have visited the fairy realm always report observing singing, dancing, and feasting.

THE FAIRY GODMOTHER

Some folklorists believe that the concept of the fairy godmother evolved from lore associated with the three Fates. It was said that the Fates came to a person when he or she was born, became a parent, and when he or she died. In Italian fairy tales the fairy godmother is often the departed spirit of a mother who returns to protect or aid her children. The original Italian story of Cinderella is one example.

In essence the fairy godmother is a guardian spirit from the Otherworld. She offers protection, assistance, and guidance to those with whom she associates. The Befana figure of Italy, a benevolent Witch who gives gifts to children and fills their stockings with treats, is a type of fairy godmother figure. Her lore is that of an ancestral spirit, thus connecting her to the Otherworld.

On the night of January 6, Befana leaves presents in children's stockings hung upon the hearth, a tradition very much like the Santa Claus tradition associated with Christmas in America. The stockings hung for Befana on the hearth are derived from ancient offerings to the goddesses of Fate and Time. Such goddesses have always been associated with weaving, the loom, the spindle and distaff. The stockings themselves are totems of goddesses associated with Fate and with weaving.

Befana is also connected to ancestral spirits as a mythical ancestress who returns yearly. Through her timeless visits to the family hearth, her function is that of reaffirming the bond between the family and the ancestors through an exchange of gifts. The children receive gifts from Befana, which in ancient times were representations of one's ancestors, for whom offerings of food were set near the hearth (very much like cookies and milk are set out for Santa Claus).

The Befana figure of Italy, a benevolent Witch who brings gifts to children, is a type of fairy godmother figure.

FAIRY TALES

In this section I have included some tales demonstrating the different views of the relationship between humankind and the fairy folk. In the oldest tales, fairies were both feared and admired by humans. When treated with respect fairies were usually kind, but fairies were very sensitive and easily offended. Fairy ethics were unlike the human kind. Fairies were well-known for taking objects from human households, and on occasion even taking an occupant of the home with them. However, fairies did not tolerate the same treatment by humans.

Fairies appear to be well disposed toward humans who offer gifts and provide various services for them. There are also stories in which a fairy and a human become lovers. However, in some tales we find that fairies cannot always be trusted, and things are not always as they seem.

THE MAIDEN AND THE FOUNTAIN FAIRY
(Scotland)

Long, long ago a drover courted and married the miller of Cuthilldorie's only daughter. The drover learned how to grind the corn, and so he set up with his young wife as the miller of Cuthilldorie when the old miller died. They did not have very much money to begin with, but an old Highlander lent them some silver, and soon they did well.

By and by the young miller and his wife had a daughter, but on the very night she was born the fairies stole her away. The wee thing was carried far away from the house into the wood of Cuthilldorie, where she was found on the very lip of the Black Well. In the air was heard a lilting:

> O we'll come back again, my honey, my hert,
> We'll come back again, my ain kind dearie;
> And you will mind upon a time
> When we met in the wood at the Well so wearie!

The lassie grew up to be by far the bonniest lass in all the countryside. Everything went well at the mill. One dark night there came a woodcock with a glowing tinder in its beak, and set fire to the mill. Everything was burnt and the miller and his wife were left without a thing in the world. To make matters worse, who should come along next day but the old Highlander who had lent them the silver, demanding payment.

Now, there was a wee old man in the wood of Cuthilldorie, beside the Black Well, who would never stay in a house if he could help it. In the winter he went away, nobody knew where. He was an ugly goblin, not more than two and a half feet high. He had been seen only three times in fifteen years since he came to the place, for he always flew up out of sight when anybody came near him. But if you crept cannily through the wood after dark, you might have heard him playing with the water, and singing the same song:

> *O when will you come, my honey, my hert,*
> *O when will you come, my ain kind dearie;*
> *For don't you mind upon the time*
> *We met in the wood at the Well so wearie?*

Well, the night after the firing of the mill, the miller's daughter wandered into the wood alone, and wandered and wandered till she came to the Black Well. Then the wee goblin gripped her and jumped about, singing:

> *O come with me, my honey, my hert,*
> *O come with me, my ain kind dearie;*
> *For don't you mind upon the time*
> *We met in the wood at the Well so wearie?*

With that he made her drink three double handfuls of witched water, and away they flew on a flash of lightning. When the poor lass opened her eyes, she was in a palace, all gold and silver and diamonds, and full of fairies. The King and Queen of the Fairies invited her to stay, and said she would be well looked after. But if she wanted to go home again, she must never tell anybody where she had been or what she had seen. She said she wanted to go home, and promised to do as she was told. Then the King said:

"The first stranger you meet, give him oatmeal."

"Give him oatcakes," said the Queen.

"Give him butter," said her King.

"Give him a drink of the Black Well water," they both said.

Then they gave her twelve drops of liquid in a wee green bottle, three drops for the oatmeal, three for the oatcakes, three for the butter and three for the Black Well water.

She took the green bottle in her hand, and suddenly it was dark. She was flying through the air, and when she opened her eyes she was at her own doorstep. She slipped away to bed, glad to be home again, and said nothing about where she had been or what she had seen.

Next morning, before the sun was up, there came a rap, rap, rap, three times at the door. The sleepy lass looked out and saw an old beggar man, who began to sing:

> *O open the door, my honey, my hert,*
> *O open the door, my ain kind dearie;*
> *For don't you mind upon the time*
> *We met in the wood at the Well so wearie?*

When she heard that, she said nothing, and opened the door. The old beggar came in singing:

> *O gie me my oatmeal, my honey, my hert,*
> *O gie me my oatmeal, my ain hind dearie;*

For don't you mind upon the time
We met in the wood at the Well so wearie?

The lassie made a bowl of oatmeal for the beggar, not forgetting the three drops of water from the green bottle. As he was supping the meal the old beggar vanished, and there in his place was the big Highlander who had lent silver to her father, the miller, and he was singing:

O gie me my oatcakes, my honey, my hert,
O gie me my oatcakes, my ain kind dearie;
For don't you mind upon the time
We met in the wood at the Well so wearie?

She baked him some fresh oatcakes, not forgetting the three drops from the wee green bottle. He had just finished eating the oatcakes when he vanished, and there in his place was the woodcock that had fired the mill, singing:

O gie me my butter, my honey, my hert,
O gie me my butter, my ain kind dearie;
For don't you mind upon the time
We met in the wood by the Well
*   so wearie?*

She gave him butter as fast as she could, not forgetting the three drops of water from the green bottle. He had only eaten a bite, when he flapped his wings and vanished, and there was the ugly wee goblin that had grabbed her at the Black Well the night before, and he was singing:

O gie me my water, my honey, my hert,
O gie me my water, my ain kind dearie;
For don't you mind upon the time
We met in the wood by the Well so wearie?

She knew there were only three other drops of water left in the green bottle and she was afraid. She ran fast as she could to the Black Well, but who should be there before her but the wee ugly goblin himself, singing:

O gie me my water, my honey, my hert,
O gie me my water, my ain kind dearie;
For don't you mind upon the time
We met in the wood by the Well so wearie?

She gave him the water, not forgetting the three drops from the green bottle. But he had scarcely drunk the witched water when he vanished, and there was a fine young Prince, who spoke to her as if he had known her all her days.

They sat down beside the Black Well.

"I was born the same night as you," he said, "and I was carried away by the fairies the same night as you were found on the lip of the Well. I was a goblin for so many years because the fairies were scared away. They made me play many tricks before they would let me go and return to my father, the King of France, and make the bonniest lass in all the world my bride."

"Who is she?" asked the maiden.

"The miller of Cuthilldorie's daughter," said the young Prince.

Then they went home and told their stories over again, and that very night they were married. A coach and four came for them, and the miller and his wife, and the Prince and the Princess, drove away singing:

O but we're happy, my honey, my hert,
O but we're happy, my ain kind dearie;

For don't you mind upon the time
We met in the wood at the Well so wearie?

—*The Lure of the Kelpie: Fairy and Folk Tales of the Highlands*
Helen Drever (Edinburgh: The Moray Press, 1937)

THE SMITH AND THE FAIRIES

Years ago there lived in Crossbrig a smith of the name of MacEachern. This man had an only child, a boy of about thirteen or fourteen years of age, cheerful, strong, and healthy. All of a sudden he fell ill, took to his bed, and moped whole days away. No one could tell what was the matter with him, and the boy himself could not, or would not, tell how he felt. He was wasting away fast; getting thin, old, and yellow; and his father and all his friends were afraid that he would die.

At last one day, after the boy had been lying in this condition for a long time, getting neither better nor worse, always confined to bed, but with an extraordinary appetite, while sadly revolving these things, and standing idly at his forge, with no heart to work, the smith was agreeably surprised to see an old man, well known to him for his sagacity and knowledge of out-of-the-way things, walk into his workshop. Forthwith he told him the occurrence which had clouded his life.

The old man looked grave as he listened; and after sitting a long time pondering over all he had heard, gave his opinion thus: "It is not your son you have got. The boy has been carried away by the 'Daoine Sith,' and they have left a *Sibhreach* in his place."

"Alas! and what then am I to do?" said the smith. "How am I ever to see my own son again?"

"I will tell you how," answered the old man. "But, first, to make sure that it is not your own son you have got, take as many empty eggshells as you can get, go with them into the room, spread them out carefully before his sight, then proceed to draw water with them, carrying them two and two in your hands as if they were a great weight, and arrange when full, with every sort of earnestness, round the fire." The smith accordingly gathered as many broken eggshells as he could get, went into the room, and proceeded to carry out all his instructions.

He had not been long at work before there arose from the bed a shout of laughter, and the voice of the seeming sick boy exclaimed, "I am now 800 years of age, and I have never seen the like of that before."

The smith returned and told the old man. "Well, now," said the sage to him, "did I not tell you that it was not your son you had: your son is in Brorra-cheill in a *digh* there (that is, a round green hill frequented by fairies). Get rid as soon as possible of this intruder, and I think I may promise you your son.

"You must light a very large and bright fire before the bed on which this stranger is lying. He will ask you, 'What is the use of such a fire as that?' Answer him at once, 'You will see that presently!' and then seize him, and throw him into the middle of it. If it is your own son you have got, he will call out to save him; but if not, this thing will fly through the roof."

The smith again followed the old man's advice; kindled a large fire, answered the question put to him as he had been directed to do, and seizing the child, flung him in without hesitation. The "Sibhreach" gave an awful yell, and sprang through the roof, where a hole was left to let the smoke out.

On a certain night the old man told him the green round hill, where the fairies kept the boy, would be open. And on that night the smith, having provided himself with a Bible, a dirk, and a crowing cock, was to proceed to the hill. He would hear singing and dancing and much merriment going on, but he was to advance boldly; the Bible he carried would be a certain safeguard to him against any danger from the fairies. On entering the hill he was to stick the dirk in the threshold, to prevent the hill from closing upon him; "and then," continued the old man, "on entering you will see a spacious apartment before you, beautifully clean, and there, standing far within, working at a forge, you will also see your own son. When you are questioned, say you come to seek him, and will not go without him."

Not long after this the time came round, and the smith sallied forth, prepared as instructed. Sure enough, as he approached the hill, there was a light where light was seldom seen before. Soon after a sound of piping, dancing, and joyous merriment reached the anxious father on the night wind.

Overcoming every impulse to fear, the smith approached the threshold steadily, stuck the dirk into it as directed, and entered. Protected by the Bible he carried on his breast, the fairies could not touch him; but they asked him, with a good deal of displeasure, what he wanted there. He answered, "I want my son, whom I see down there, and I will not go without him."

Upon hearing this the whole company before him gave a loud laugh, which wakened the cock he carried dozing in his arms, who at once leaped up on his shoulder, clapped his wings lustily, and crowed loud and long.

The fairies, incensed, seized the smith and his son, and, throwing them out of the hill, flung the dirk after them. In an instant all was dark.

For a year and a day the boy never did a turn of work, and hardly ever spoke a word; but at last one day, sitting by his father and watching him finishing a sword he was making for some chief, and which he was very particular about, he suddenly exclaimed, "That is not the way to do it"; and, taking the tools from his father's hands, he set to work himself in his place, and soon fashioned a sword the like of which was never seen in the country before.

From that day the young man wrought constantly with his father, and became the inventor of a peculiarly fine and well-tempered weapon, the making of which kept the two smiths, father and son, in constant employment, spread their fame far and wide, and gave them the means in abundance, as they before had the disposition, to live content with all the world and very happily with one another.

—*Popular Tales of the West Highlands: Scottish Fairy and Folk Tales*
J. F. Campbell (London: Walter Scott Publishing Co., 1901), pp. 125–128

The Walnut Fairies
(Italy)

There was at Benevento a poor family whose members gained their living by going about the country and getting fruit, which they sold. One day the youngest son was roaming, trying to see what he could find, when he beheld a walnut tree—but one so beautiful 'twas hardly credible what nuts were on it! Truly he thought he had a good thing of it, but as he gathered the nuts they opened, and from every one came a beautiful little lady who at once grew to life size. They were gay and merry, and so fair they seemed the eyes of the sun. Sweet music sounded from the leaves, they made him dance; 'twas a fine festa.

But he did not for all that forget why he had come there, and that the family at home wanted bread. But the ladies, who were fairies (fate), knew this, and when the dancing was over they gave him some of the nuts. And they said: "When you shall be at home open two of these, keep a third for the king's daughter, and take this little basket full to the king. And tell the queen's daughter not to open her walnut till she shall have gone to bed."

And when he had returned and opened his nut there poured from it such a stream of gold that he found himself richer than the king. So he built himself a castle of extraordinary splendor, all of precious stones.

And opening the second nut there came from it such a magnificent suit of clothes that when he put it on he was the handsomest man in the world. So he went to the king and was well received. However, when he asked for the hand of the princess, the monarch replied that he was very sorry, but he had promised his daughter to another prince. For this other prince the princess had no love at all, but she was enamored with the youth.

So she accepted the nut, and went to bed, but oh what wonder! What should come out of it but the young man who had asked her in marriage! Now as she could not help herself, and moreover, had no special desire to be helped, she made the best of it, and suffered him only to remain, but to return, which he did zealously, full many a time; with the natural result

that in the course of events the princess found herself with child, and declared that something must be done.

And this was arranged. She went to her father and said that she would never marry the prince to whom he had betrothed her, and that there should be a grand assembly of youths, and they should agree that, let her choose whom she would, they would support her choice. So it was done, and there were feasts, balls, and at last a great assembly of young men. Among them appeared her own lover, the man of the walnuts. And he was dressed like a poor peasant, and sat at the table among the humblest who were there. The princess went forth from one to the other of those who wished to marry her. And she found some fault in every one, till she came to her own lover, and said: "That is the one who I choose," and threw her handkerchief at him—which was a sign that she would marry him.

Then all who were present were enraged that she should have selected such a peasant, or beggar, nor was the king himself well pleased. At last it was arranged that there should be a combat, and that if the young man could hold his own in the might marry the princess. Now he was strong and brave, yet this was a great trial. But the Ladies of the Walnut Tree helped their friend, so that all fell before him. Never a sword or lance touched him in the fray, he bore a charmed life, and the opposing knights went down before him like sheep before a wolf. He was the victor and wedded the daughter of the king; and after a few months she gave birth to a beautiful babe who was called, in gratitude to the fairy ladies, the Walnut of Benevento. And so they were happy and contented.

—*Etruscan Roman Remains*
Charles Leland (London: T. Fischer Unwin, 1892), pp. 193–195.

THE ELVES AND THE SHOEMAKER
(England)

There was once a shoemaker who, through no fault of his own, had become so poor that at last he had only leather enough left for one pair of shoes. At evening he cut out the shoes which he intended to begin upon the next morning, and since he had a good conscience, he lay down quietly, said his prayers, and fell asleep.

In the morning when he had prayed, as usual, and was preparing to sit down to work, he found the pair of shoes standing finished on his table. He was amazed, and could not understand it in the least. He took the shoes in his hand to examine them more closely.

They were so neatly sewn that not a stitch was out of place, and were as good as the work of a master-hand. Soon after a purchaser came in, and as he was much pleased with the shoes, he paid more than the ordinary price for them, so that the shoemaker was able to buy leather for two pairs with the money.

He cut them out in the evening, and next day, with fresh courage was about to go to work; but he had no need to, for when he got up, the shoes were finished, and buyers were not lacking. These gave him so much money that he was able to buy leather for four pairs of shoes. Early next morning he found the four pairs finished, and so it went on; what he cut out at evening was finished in the morning, so that he was soon again in comfortable circumstances, and became a well-to-do man.

Now it happened one evening, not long before Christmas, when he had cut out shoes as usual, that he said to his wife: "How would it be if we were to sit up tonight to see who it is that lends us such a helping hand?" The wife agreed, lighted a candle, and they hid themselves in the corner of the room behind the clothes that were hanging there.

At midnight came two little naked men, who sat down at the shoemaker's table, took up the cut-out work, and began with their tiny fingers to stitch, sew, and hammer so neatly and quickly, that the shoemaker could not believe his eyes. They did not stop till everything was quite finished, and stood complete on the table; then they ran swiftly away.

The next day the wife said: "The little men have made us rich, and we ought to show our gratitude. They run about with nothing on, and must freeze with cold. Now I will make them little shirts, coats, waistcoats, and hose, and will even knit them stout stockings, and you shall make them each a pair of shoes." The husband agreed, and at evening, when they had everything ready, they laid out the presents on the table, and hid themselves to see how the little men would behave.

At midnight the little men came skipping in, and were about to set to work; but instead of the leather ready cut out, they found the charming little clothes. At first they were surprised, then excessively delighted. With the greatest speed they put on and smoothed down the pretty clothes, singing: "Now we're dressed so fine and neat, why cobble more for others' feet?" Then they hopped and danced about, and leaped over chairs and tables and out at the door. Henceforward, they came back no more, but the shoemaker fared well as long as he lived, and had good luck in all his undertakings.

—*The Young Folks Treasury,* Volume 1
(The University Society Inc., 1909)

THE LEGEND OF KNOCKGRAFTON
(Ireland)

There was once a poor man who lived in the fertile glen of Aherlow, at the foot of the gloomy Galtee mountains, and he had a great hump on his back: he looked just as if his body had been rolled up and placed upon his shoulders; and his head was pressed down with the weight so much that his chin, when he was sitting, used to rest upon his knees for support.

The country people were rather shy of meeting him in any lonesome place, for though, poor creature, he was as harmless and as inoffensive as a newborn infant, yet his deformity was so great that he scarcely appeared to be a human creature, and some ill-minded persons had set strange stories about him afloat. He was said to have a great knowledge of herbs and charms; but certain it was that he had a mighty skillful hand in plaiting straw and rushes into hats and baskets, which was the way he made his livelihood.

Lusmore, for that was the nickname put upon him by reason of his always wearing a sprig of the fairy cap, or lusmore (the foxglove), in his little straw hat, would ever get a higher penny for his plaited work than any one else, and perhaps that was the reason why some one, out of envy, had circulated the strange stories about him. Be that as it may, it happened that he was returning one evening from the pretty town of Cahir toward Cappagh, and as little Lusmore walked very slowly, on account of the great hump upon his back, it was quite dark when he came to the old moat of Knockgrafton, which stood on the right-hand side of his road.

Tired and weary was he, and noways comfortable in his own mind at thinking how much farther he had to travel, and that he should be walking all the night; so he sat down under the moat to rest himself, and began looking mournfully enough upon the moon.

Presently there rose a wild strain of unearthly melody upon the ear of little Lusmore; he listened, and he thought that he had never heard such ravishing music before. It was like the sound of many voices, each mingling and blending with the other so strangely that they seemed to be one, though all singing different strains, and the words of the song were these: "*Da Luan, Da Mort, Da Luan, Da Mort, Da Luan, Da Mort*"; then there would be a moment's pause, and then the round of melody went on again.

Lusmore listened attentively, scarcely drawing his breath lest he might lose the slightest note. He now plainly perceived that the singing was within the moat; and though at first it had charmed him so much, he began to get tired of hearing the same round sung over and over so often without any change; so availing himself of the pause when the "*Da Luan, Da Mort*" had been sung three times, he took up the tune, and raised it with the words "*augus Da Cadine*," and then went on singing with the voices inside of the moat, "*Da Luan, Da Mort*," finishing the melody, when the pause again came, with "*augus Da Cadine*."

The fairies within Knockgrafton, for the song was a fairy melody, when they heard this addition to the tune, were so much delighted that, with instant resolve, it was determined to bring the mortal among them, whose musical skill so far exceeded theirs, and little Lusmore was conveyed into their company with the eddying speed of a whirlwind.

Glorious to behold was the sight that burst upon him as he came down through the moat, twirling round and round, with the lightness of a straw, to the sweetest music that kept time to his motion. The greatest honor was then paid him, for he was put above all the musicians, and he had servants tending upon him, and everything to his heart's content, and a hearty welcome to all; and, in short, he was made as much of as if he had been the first man in the land.

Presently Lusmore saw a great consultation going forward among the fairies, and, notwithstanding all their civility, he felt very much frightened, until one stepping out from the rest came up to him and said:

Lusmore! Lusmore!
Doubt not, nor deplore,
For the hump which you bore
On your back is no more;
Look down on the floor,
And view it, Lusmore!

When these words were said, poor little Lusmore felt himself so light, and so happy, that he thought he could have bounded at one jump over the moon, like the cow in the history of the cat and the fiddle; and he saw, with inexpressible pleasure, his hump tumble down upon the ground from his shoulders. He then tried to lift up his head, and he did so with becoming caution, fearing that he might knock it against the ceiling of the grand hall, where he was; he looked round and round again with greatest wonder and delight upon everything, which appeared more and more beautiful; and, overpowered at beholding such a resplendent scene, his head grew dizzy, and his eyesight became dim.

At last he fell into a sound sleep, and when he awoke he found that it was broad daylight, the sun shining brightly, and the birds singing sweetly; and that he was lying just at the foot of the moat of Knockgrafton, with the cows and sheep grazing peacefully round about him. The first thing Lusmore did, after saying his prayers, was to put his hand behind to feel for his hump, but no sign of one was there on his back, and he looked at himself with great pride, for he had now become a well-shaped, dapper little fellow, and more than that, found himself in a full suit of new clothes, which he concluded the fairies had made for him.

Toward Cappagh he went, stepping out as lightly, and springing up at every step as if he had been all his life a dancing-master. Not a creature who met Lusmore knew him without his hump, and he had a great work to persuade every one that he was the same man—in truth he was not, so far as outward appearance went.

Of course it was not long before the story of Lusmore's hump got about, and a great wonder was made of it. Through the country, for miles round, it was the talk of every one, high and low.

One morning, as Lusmore was sitting contented enough, at his cabin door, up came an old woman to him, and asked him if he could direct her to Cappagh.

"I need give you no directions, my good woman," said Lusmore, "for this is Cappagh; and whom may you want here?"

"I have come," said the woman, "out of Decie's country, in the county of Waterford, looking after one Lusmore, who, I have heard tell, had his hump taken off by the fairies; for there is a son of a gossip of mine who has got a hump on him that will be his death; and maybe if he could use the same charm as Lusmore, the hump may be taken off him. And now I have told you the reason of my coming so far: 'tis to find out about this charm, if I can."

Lusmore, who was ever a good-natured little fellow, told the woman all the particulars, how he had raised the tune for the fairies at Knockgrafton, how his hump had been removed from his shoulders, and how he had got a new suit of clothes into the bargain.

The woman thanked him very much, and then went away quite happy and easy in her own mind. When she came back to her gossip's house, in the county of Waterford, she told her everything that Lusmore had said, and they put the little hump-backed man, who was a peevish and cunning creature from his birth, upon a car, and took him all the way across the country. It was a long journey, but they did not care for that, so the hump was taken from off him; and they brought him, just at nightfall, and left him under the old moat of Knockgrafton.

Jack Madden, for that was the humpy man's name, had not been sitting there long when he heard the tune going on within the moat much sweeter than before; for the fairies were singing it the way Lusmore had settled their music for them, and the song was going on; "*Da Luan, Da Mort, Da*

Luan, Da Mort, Da Luan, Da Mort, augus Da Cadine," without ever stopping.

Jack Madden, who was in a great hurry to get quit of his hump, never thought of waiting until the fairies had done, or watching for a fit opportunity to raise the tune higher again than Lusmore had; so having heard them sing it over seven times without stopping, out he bawls, never minding the time or the humor of the tune, or how he could bring his words in properly, "*augus Da Cadine, augus Da Hena,*" thinking that if one day was good, two were better; and that if Lusmore had one new suit of clothes given him, he should have two.

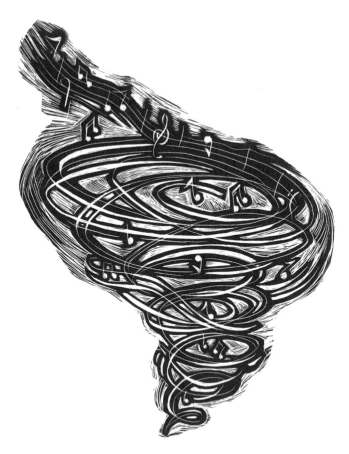

No sooner had the words passed his lips than he was taken up and whisked into the moat with prodigious force; and the fairies came crowding round about him with great anger, screeching and screaming, and roaring out, "Who spoiled our tune? Who spoiled our tune?" and one stepped up to him, above all the rest and said:

Jack Madden! Jack Madden!
Your words came so bad in
The tune we felt glad in;
This castle you're had in,
That your life we may sadden;
Here's two humps for Jack Madden!

And twenty of the strongest fairies brought Lusmore's hump and put it down upon poor Jack's back, over his own, where it became fixed as firmly as if it was nailed on with twelve-penny nails, by the best carpenter that ever drove one. Out of their castle they then kicked him; and, in the morning, when Jack Madden's mother and her gossip came to look after their little man, they found him half dead, lying at the foot of the moat, with the other hump upon his back. Well to be sure, how they did look at each other! But they were afraid to say anything, lest a hump might be put upon their own shoulders. Home they brought the unlucky Jack Madden with them, as downcast in their hearts and their looks as ever two gossips were; and what through the weight of his other hump, and the long journey, he died soon after, leaving, they say, his heavy curse to anyone who would go to listen to fairy tunes again.

—*More Celtic Fairy Tales*
Joseph Jacobs (London: David Nutt, 1894), pp. 156–163

THE RED-HAIRED TAILOR OF RANNOCH AND THE FAIRY

The red-haired tailor lived in Rannoch. Like the rest of his kind, he went from house to house to make clothes of the cloth which thrifty wives manufactured for their husbands and sons in bygone times.

Once as he was approaching a house, where he had a few days' work to do, evening came on, and he saw, in the dimness of the twilight, one like a very little child, running before him and keeping out of sight behind every bush and every hillock at the roadside. The tailor hardened his step, hoping to overtake the curious manikin before him, but instead of gaining, he was losing ground at every step he took. As soon as he noticed this, he began to run with all his might; but in spite of his skin, he could not shorten the distance between them.

At length he lost patience so completely that he threw his big shears at the nimble little man ahead, and struck him with them in the knee joints. The fairy, for such he was, fell on his face, and before he had time to rise up, was in the tailor's arms, and the shears on his breast.

"Tell me where thou art going, my good lad," said the tailor.

"I am on my way from the Big Fairy Knoll, to the house ahead of thee, to get a while of the breast of the wife," replied the little imp. This was the very house to which the tailor was going.

"And what wilt thou do with the woman's own child?" said the tailor then.

"Oh, I will put him out at the back window to my people, and they will take him with them to our place," answered the other.

"And will they send him home when thou hast had enough of his mother's breast?"

"Oh, no; never!"

"That will do," said the tailor, and he let his prisoner go.

As soon as he got his liberty, he stretched away to the house, and was within before the tailor arrived. He had the house to himself, for the good man and his wife were in the byre milking the cows, and no one within but the child in the cradle. He lifted the child in his arms, and handed it out at the back window to the other fairies, as he thought; but the tailor was before them, and took the child quietly in his arms, and then went away with it to the house of his sister, who lived a short distance off, and left it in her charge.

When he returned he found the wife before him, and the changeling in the cradle, ready to burst with crying. The wife took him up, and gave him a drink, and then put him back in the cradle again.

He was not long there until he began to scream and cry once more. She took him up, and gave him another drink. But to all appearance nothing would please him but to be left always on the breast.

This game went on for a few days more. But when the patience of the tailor ran out, he sprang at last from the work-table, took in a creelful of peats, and put a big fire on the hearth. When the fire was in the heat of its burning, he sprang over to the cradle, took with him the changeling, and before any one in the house could interpose, he threw him into the very middle of the flames. But the little knave leaped out through the chimney, and from the housetop cried in triumph to the wife: "I have got so much of the sap of thy breast in spite of thee," and he departed.

—*Folk Tales and Fairy Lore in Gaelic and English*
James MacDougall (Edinburgh: John Grant, 1910), pp. 142–147

THE TWO HUMPBACKS
(Italy)

There were once two companions who were humpbacks, but one more so than the other. They were both so poor that they had not a penny to their names. One of them said: "I will go out into the world, for here there is nothing to eat; we are dying of hunger. I want to see whether I can make my fortune."

"Go," said the other. "If you make your fortune, return, and I will go and see if I can make mine."

So the humpback set off on his journey. Now these two humpbacks were from Parma. When the humpback had gone a long way, he came to a square where there was a fair, at which everything was sold.

There was a person selling cheese, who cried out: "Eat the little Parmesan!" The poor humpback thought he meant him, so he ran away and hid

himself in a courtyard. When it was one o'clock, he heard a clanking of chains and the words "Saturday and Sunday" repeated several times.

Then he answered: "And Monday."

"Oh, heavens!" said they who were singing. "Who is this who has harmonized with our choir?"

They searched and found the poor humpback hidden.

"Oh gentlemen!" he said, "I have not come here to do any harm, you know!"

"Well! We have come to reward you; you have harmonized our choir; come with us!" They put him on a table and removed his hump, healed him, and gave him two bags of money.

"Now," they said, "you can go." He thanked them and went away without his hump. He liked it better, you can believe! He returned to his place at Parma, and when the other humpback saw him he exclaimed: "Does not that look just like my friend? But he had a hump! It is not he! Listen! You are not my friend so and so, are you?"

"Yes, I am," he replied.

"Listen! Were you not a humpback?"

"Yes. They have removed my hump and given me two bags of money. I will tell you why. I reached," he continued, "such and such a place, and I heard them beginning to say, 'Eat the little Parmesan! Eat the little Parmesan!' I was so frightened that I hid myself." (He mentioned the place—in a courtyard.) "At a certain hour, I heard a noise of chains and a chorus singing: 'Saturday and Sunday.' After two or three times, I said: 'And Monday.' They came and found me, saying that I had harmonized their chorus, and they wanted to reward me. They took me, removed my hump, and gave me two bags of money."

"Oh, heavens!" said the other humpback. "I want to go there, too!"

"Go, poor fellow, go! Farewell!"

The humpback reached the place, and hid himself precisely where his companion had. After a while he heard a noise of chains, and the chorus:

"Saturday and Sunday!" Then another chorus: "And Monday!" After the humpback had heard them repeat: "Saturday and Sunday, and Monday!" several times, he added: "And Tuesday!"

"Where," they exclaimed, "is he who has spoiled our chorus? If we find him, we will tear him in pieces." Just think! They struck and beat this poor humpback until they were tired; then they put him on the same table on which they had placed his companion, and said: "Take that hump and put it on him in front."

So they took the other's hump and fastened it to his breast, and then drove him away with blows. He went home and found his friend, who cried: "Mercy! Is not that my friend? But it cannot be, for this one is humpbacked in front. Listen," he said, "are you not my friend?"

"The same," he answered, weeping. "I did not want to bear my own hump, and now I have to carry mine and yours! And so beaten and reduced, you see!"

"Come," said his friend, "come home with me, and we will eat a mouthful together; and don't be disheartened."

And so, every day, he dined with his friend, and afterward they died, I imagine.

—*Italian Popular Tales*
Thomas Frederick Crane
(New York: Houghton Mifflin and Company, 1883), pp. 103–104.

The Recovered Bride
(Ireland)

There was a marriage in the townland of Curragraigue. After the usual festivities, and when the guests were left to themselves, and were drinking to the prosperity of the bride and bridegroom, they were startled by the appearance of the man himself rushing into the room with anguish in his looks.

"Oh!" cried he, "Margaret is carried away by the fairies, I'm sure. The girls were not left the room for half a minute when I went in, and there is no more sign of her there than if she never was born."

Great consternation prevailed, great search was made, but no Margaret was to be found. After a night and day spent in misery, the poor bridegroom laid down to take some rest. In a while he seemed to himself to awake from a troubled dream, and look out into the room. The moon was shining in through the window, and in the middle of the slanting rays stood Margaret in her white bridal clothes. He thought to speak and leap out of the bed, but his tongue was without utterance, and his limbs unable to move.

"Do not be disturbed, dear husband," said the appearance; "I am now in the power of the fairies, but if you only have courage and prudence we may be soon happy with each other again. Next Friday will be May-eve, and the whole court will ride out of the old fort after midnight. I must be there along with the rest. Sprinkle a circle with holy water, and have a black-hafted knife with you. If you have courage to pull me off the horse, and draw me into the ring, all they can do will be useless. You must have some food for me every night on the dresser, for if I taste one mouthful with them, I will be lost to you forever. The fairies got power over me because I was only thinking of you, and did not prepare myself as I ought for the sacrament. I made a bad confession, and now I am suffering for it. Don't forget what I have said."

"Oh, no, my darling," cried he, recovering his speech, but by the time he had slipped out of bed, there was no living soul in the room but himself.

Until Friday night the poor young husband spent a desolate time. The food was left on the dresser over night, and it rejoiced all hearts to find it vanished by morning. A little before midnight he was at the entrance of the old rath. He formed the circle, took his station within it, and kept the black-hafted knife ready for service. At times he was nervously afraid of losing his dear wife, and at others burning with impatience for the struggle.

At last the old fort with its dark, high bushy fences cutting against the sky, was in a moment replaced by a palace and its court. A thousand lights flashed from the windows and lofty hall entrance; numerous torches were brandished by attendants stationed around the courtyard; and a numerous cavalcade of richly attired ladies and gentlemen was moving in the direction of the gate where he found himself standing.

As they rode by him, laughing and jesting, he could not tell whether they were aware of his presence or not. He looked intently at each countenance as it approached, but it was some time before he caught sight of the dear face and figure borne along on a milk-white steed. She recognized him well enough, and her features now broke into a smile—now expressed deep anxiety.

She was unable for the throng to guide the animal close to the ring of power; so he suddenly rushed out of his bounds, seized her in his arms, and lifted her off. Cries of rage and fury arose on every side; they were hemmed in, and weapons were directed at his head and breast to terrify him. He seemed to be inspired with superhuman courage and force, and wielding the powerful knife he soon cleared a space round him, all seeming dismayed by the sight of the weapon. He lost no time, but drew his wife within the ring, within which none of the myriads around dared to enter. Shouts of derision and defiance continued to fill the air for some time, but the expedition could not be delayed.

As the end of the procession filed past the gate and the circle within which the mortal pair held each other determinedly clasped, darkness and silence fell on the old rath and the fields round it, and the rescued bride and her lover breathed freely.

We will not detain the sensitive reader on the happy walk home, on the joy that hailed their arrival, and on all the eager gossip that occupied the townland and the five that surround it for a month after the happy rescue.

—*Legendary Fictions of the Irish Celts*
Patrick Kennedy (London: Macmillan and Company, 1866), pp. 111–113

THE FAIRIES' HILL
(Scotland)

There is a green hill above Kintraw, known as the Fairies' Hill, of which the following story is told. Many years ago, the wife of the farmer at Kintraw fell ill and died, leaving two or three young children. The Sunday after the funeral the farmer and his servants went to church, leaving the children at home in charge of the eldest, a girl of about ten years of age. On the farmer's return the children told him their mother had been to see them, and had combed their hair and dressed them. As they still persisted in their statement after being remonstrated with, they were punished for telling what was not true.

The following Sunday the same thing occurred again. The father now told the children, if their mother came again, they were to inquire of her why she came. Next Sunday, when she reappeared, the eldest child put her father's question to her, when the mother told them she had been carried off by the "Good People" (Daione Sidth), and could only get away for an hour or two on Sundays, and should her coffin be opened it would be found to contain only a withered leaf.

The farmer, much perplexed, went to the minister for advice, who scoffed at the idea of any supernatural connection with the children's story, ridiculed the existence of "Good People," and would not allow the coffin to be opened. The matter was therefore allowed to rest. But, some little time after, the minister, who had gone to Lochgilphead for the day, was found lying dead near the Fairies' Hill, a victim, many people thought, of the indignation of the Fairy world at which he had laughed.

—*Waifs and Strays of Celtic Tradition,* Argyllshire Series, vol. 1
Lord Archibald Campbell (London: David Nutt, 1889), pp. 71–72

THE STOLEN LADY
(Scotland)

John Roy, who lived in Glenbroun, in the parish of Abernethy, being out one night on the hills in search of his cattle, met a troop of fairies, who seemed to have got a prize of some sort or other. Recollecting that the fairies are obliged to exchange whatever they may have with any one who offers them anything, however low in value, for it, he flung his bonnet to them, crying "*Shuis slo slumus sheen*" (i.e., "mine is yours and yours is mine"). The fairies dropped their booty, which proved to be a Sassenach (English) lady whom the dwellers of Shian of Coir-laggac had carried away from her own country, leaving a stock in her place which, of course, died and was buried.

John brought her home, and she lived for many years in his house. "It happened, however, in the course of time," said the Gaelic narrator, "that the new king found it necessary to make the great roads through these countries by means of soldiers, for the purpose of letting coaches and carriages pass to the northern cities; and those soldiers had officers and commanders in the same way as our fighting army have now. Those soldiers were never great favorites in these countries, particularly during the time that our kings were alive; and consequently it was no easy matter for them, either officers or men, to procure for themselves comfortable quarters."

But John Roy would not keep up the national animosity to the *cottan dearg* (red-coats), and he offered a residence in his house to a Saxon captain and his son. When there they could not take their eyes off the English lady, and the son remarked to his father what a strong likeness she bore to his deceased mother.

The father replied that he too had been struck with the resemblance, and said he could almost fancy she was his wife. He then mentioned her name and those of some persons connected with them. The lady by these words at once recognized her husband and son, and honest John Roy had the satisfaction of reuniting the long-separated husband and wife, and receiving their most grateful acknowledgments.

—*The Fairy Mythology: Illustrative of the Romance and Superstition of Various Countries*
Thomas Keightley (London: H. G. Bohn, 1850), pp. 391–392.

BREWERY OF EGGSHELLS

In Treneglwys there is a certain shepherd's cot known by the name of Twt y Cymrws, because of the strange strife that occurred there. There once lived there a man and his wife, and they had twins whom the woman nursed tenderly. One day she was called away to the house of a neighbor at some distance. She did not much like going and leaving her little ones all alone in a solitary house, especially as she had heard tell of the good folk haunting the neighborhood.

Well, she went and came back as soon as she could, but on her way back she was frightened to see some old elves of the blue petticoat crossing her path, though it was midday. She rushed home, but found her two little ones in the cradle and everything seemed as it was before.

But after a time the good people began to suspect that something was wrong, for the twins didn't grow at all.

The man said: "They're not ours."

The woman said: "Whose else should they be?"

And so arose the great strife so that the neighbors named the cottage after it. It made the woman very sad, so one evening she made up her mind to go and see the Wise Man of Llanidloes, for he knew everything and would advise her what to do.

So she went to Llanidloes and told the case to the Wise Man. Now there was soon to be a harvest of rye and oats, so the Wise Man said to her, "When you are getting dinner for the reapers, clear out the shell of a hen's egg and boil some potage in it, and then take it to the door as if you meant it as a dinner for the reapers. Then listen if the twins say anything. If you hear them speaking of things beyond the understanding of children, go back and take them up and throw them into the waters of Lake Elvyn. But if you don't hear anything remarkable, do them no injury."

So when the day of the reap came the woman did all that the Wise Man ordered, and put the eggshell on the fire and took it off and carried it to the door, and there she stood and listened. Then she heard one of the children say to the other:

> *Acorn before oak I knew,*
> *An egg before a hen,*
> *But I never heard of an eggshell brew*
> *A dinner for harvest men.*

So she went back into the house, seized the children and threw them into the Llyn, and the goblins in their blue trousers came and saved their dwarfs and the mother had her own children back and so the great strife ended.

—"Celtic Fairy Tales," by Joseph Jacobs
Cambrian Quarterly Magazine, 1830, vol. ii, p. 86

A Smith Rescues a Captured Woman from a Troll
(Denmark)

As a smith was at work in his forge late one evening, he heard great wailing out on the road, and by the light of the red-hot iron that he was hammering, he saw a woman whom a troll was driving along, bawling at her "A little more! A little more!" He ran out, put the red-hot iron between them, and thus delivered her from the power of the troll.

He led her into his house and that night she was delivered of twins. In the morning he went and attended to her husband, who he supposed must be in great affliction at the loss of his wife. But to his surprise he saw there, in bed, a woman the very image of the one he had saved from the troll. Knowing at once what she must be, he raised an axe he had in his hand, and cleft her skull. The matter was soon explained to the satisfaction of the husband, who gladly received his real wife and her twins.

—*The Fairy Mythology: Illustrative of the Romance*
and Superstition of Various Countries
Thomas Keightley (London: H. G. Bohn, 1850), p. 392

FLOWER LORE

So when you or I are made
A fable, song, or fleeting shade;
All love, all liking, all delight
Lies drown'd with us in endless night.
Then while time serves, and we are but decaying;
Come, my Corinna, come, let's go a-Maying.

—Robert Herrick

May is a season associated with buds and flowers. These reflect the theme of ever-renewing life. In the ancient Mediterranean region the month of May was sacred to Maia and Flora, goddesses associated with flowering plants. Honor was paid to these goddesses by decorating their shrines with beautiful flowers. Throughout continental Europe and the British Isles a great deal of folklore concerning flowers has evolved over the centuries. Much of this type of lore is also associated with fairies. In the Old Religion of pre-Christian Europe it was believed that fairies helped open the buds of plants and cared for all growing things in general. Fairies claimed green as their sacred color and took any offense against it quite seriously.

The old lore of Europe is rich with images of fairies gathering at night in celebrations conducted inside fairy rings (a circle of mushrooms in a forest clearing). In the book *Flower Lore*, by Hilderick Friend (Rockport: Para Research, Inc., 1981), the author speaks of the old beliefs in Devonshire that fairies used mushrooms as dinner tables. A type of fungus (a species of gelatin) sometimes grew on top of these mushrooms, and people called it "Fairy Butter." In Holywell, in Flintshire, the miners also referred to as fairy butter a substance found at great depth in crevices.

Various plants associated with fairies serve as dwelling places. Some of these are trees, while others are herbs and flowers. One of the earliest and most notable examples is the myrtle plant. It appears in several key fairy tales. In this chapter we will explore this plant, along with many others that are rich in fairy lore. Most are related to the May season. The few plants listed that are not associated with May are linked to the magick of fairies.

FLOWER MEANINGS

COWSLIP *(Primula veris)* is a flower associated with divination. One of the oldest customs was to make a ball of cowslip flowers. The ball was then tossed up and caught as it fell each time, until it either broke apart or dropped to the ground. During the process the names of various occupations were spoken in succession. When the cowslip ball broke or fell, this was believed to indicate what profession the participant would achieve. Another technique was to say "tissty-tossty tell me true, who shall I be married to," and then begin to toss the cowslip ball while calling out various names.

In the old Anglo-Saxon, cowslip was spelled *cuslyppa* or *cusloppe*. Cowslip is also known as "the fairy cup." An old folk belief held that fairies climbed into cowslip flowers to avoid the rain. This belief is linked to the ancient concept that fairies animated Nature, opening and closing flowers, making fruit grow, and so on. Many of the unseen forces of Nature were ascribed to the power of the fairy race.

DAISY *(Bellis perennis)* is a flower sometimes called the harbinger of spring. It is a flower long associated with divination. In the folk magic tradition, petals are plucked from the flower in order to obtain a yes or no answer to a question. Words such as "he/she loves me" and "he/she loves me not" are spoken as each petal is removed. The final remaining petal reveals the answer to the question.

DANDELION *(Taraxacum officinale)* is another of the divinatory flowers of folk magic. When the plant is ready to seed, a multitude of fluffy heads appear. Blowing on this causes the seeds to dislodge and the seeds to float in the air similar to a parachute. In South Kensington the floating seeds are called fairies, and it is be-lieved that to catch one in the air brings good luck. In the United States a wish is made and then the seeds are blown up into the air. This is done in the belief that the seeds will carry the wish away. The wish will then be grant-ed at a later time as the new plants grow to fullness.

ELECAMPANE *(Inula helenium)* is a plant associated with fairies. It is common throughout most of continental Europe and England. Some commentators have suggested that the name "elecampane" comes from the Danish word for fairy, which is *Elle*. The Elecampane is known by many names, such as elfwort, elfdock, horseheal, and scabwort.

In old European lore elecampane was said to possess the power to raise the dead. In folk remedies it was used to treat skin conditions of various animals such as sheep and horses. People also used the herb to cure coughs and bronchitis.

FOXGLOVE *(Digitalis purpurea)* is a magical plant long associated with fairies. In some areas of Europe foxglove plants are called fairy bells or fairy gloves. In Devonshire the foxglove was known as cowslip, which is actually another flower altogether. The foxglove plant bears beautiful purple flowers and is the source of the heart medication known as digitalis. It is a very magickal plant, complementing any garden. Among the Irish the foxglove is called the fairy-cap. The Welsh know it as *Maneg Ellylln,* the "fairies' glove." In Cheshire the foxglove is called the "fairies' petticoat" and in East Anglia it is known as "the fairy thimble."

HAWTHORN *(Crataegus spp.)* is known also as the May flower, May bush, May bloom, or May tree. In Ireland the hawthorn (called white thorn) was considered magical, and its blossoms were placed on the bedroom dresser to ward off illness. On the first of May it was once the custom to sprinkle hawthorn sprigs with holy water and to set them in the fields to protect the crops from the fairies. In some of the oldest lore the hawthorn was a protective gateway to the fairy realm.

According to some sources it was planted with the oak and ash trees, and where the three grew together one could commune with fairies. The ancient Greeks placed hawthorn blossoms on the bridal altar, and on occasion the bride sometimes carried a sprig of hawthorn to ensure a fruitful and happy marriage. The thorns of the plant were a reminder that life also includes pain. In the lore associated with May, the thorns on the boughs of hawthorn (hung over the entrance to the home) served to protect the family from evil forces. It was once the custom in many parts of Europe to adorn doors, posts, and other parts of the home with hawthorn and other flowers on May Day.

LADY'S SLIPPER *(Cypripedium pubescens)* is a member of the valerian family, having protective powers that may be used to guard against spells, hexes, curses, and the evil eye.

LADY'S SMOCK *(Cardamine pratensis)* is a flower that was once widely used in May garlands. It was also included among the flowers presented to the May Queen. Shakespeare refers to the Lady Smock in connection with the cuckoo bud and with the bird of the same name.

MARSH MARIGOLD *(Caltha palustris)* is a flower dedicated to the May Queen. In western England the marsh marigold is sometimes called horse-buttercup or bull's eyes, and in Somerset they are called Bull flowers. One of its Manx names is *Lus y Voaldyn*, the herb of Beltane. Another name by which it is known is the king-cup. In the past the marigold was strewn in front of doors and woven into garlands for the May Queen. In Ireland and on the Isle of Man the marsh marigold was believed to be a protective talisman. The flowers were picked May Eve, and on May 1 were strewn on cottage roofs to keep evil fairies away. If the marsh marigolds were not in bloom, it was considered a bad omen for the coming season.

MAY BLOSSOM is a term for several flowering plants common to the May season. Among these is the Mayflower, which is also known as hawthorn.

MAY LILY or lily of the valley *(Convallaria majalis)* is one of the flowers dedicated to the May Queen on May Day.

MYRTLE *(Myrtus communis)* appears in some of the oldest fairy lore as a very special tree sacred to fairies. In the Aegean/Mediterranean the myrtle was a symbol of immortality and life after death. In southern European lore, the myrtle tree is often the home of a fairy. The myrtle has traditionally carried with it many different associations throughout Europe. In Germany it was used to make the bridal wreath and served as a symbol of fertility and purity. In other cultures it symbolized war and sorrow. During the Middle Ages, wreaths of myrtle were given to acknowledge acts of chivalry.

STITCHWORT *(Stellaria holostea)* is a plant dedicated to the pixies, and it is included in the fairy garland. In Devonshire the plant itself was called "pixy," and it was said that fairies were particularly fond of stitchwort. Therefore, caution was urged in not picking the stitchwort as it could result in being pixie-led. To be "pixie-led" meant that one was enchanted by the fairies and then taken off to some remote spot to dance all night with them. This left the person dazed the next day, sitting lost in the forest with little memory of what transpired. Folk names connected to the stitchwort are devil's eyes and devil's corn, and White-Sunday.

WOOD SORREL *(Oxcalis acetosella)* is a plant that looks similar to the shamrock. Wood sorrel is also known as the "Welsh fairy bell." People believed that these bell-shaped flowers called the elves to moonlight dances and revelry. In some old texts the wood sorrel is also called the shamrock, along with purple clover, speedwell, and pimpernel. However, none of these plants are what today would be called the shamrock.

In old folklore the wood sorrel is said to predict a coming storm. The plant has been noted to compress its triplet of leaves when the air grows damp, and this may be the source of the legend. On a darker note, several Italian painters, such as Fra Angelico, were known to have included the wood sorrel in paintings of the crucifixion of Jesus, where it appeared in the foreground of the cross.

The Language of Flowers

By the close of the nineteenth century a standard list of flowers and their poetic meanings existed. To send someone a flower was to convey a specific sentiment. The following is a list of the most commonly attributed meanings associated with the giving of flowers.

Flower	Meaning
Arbor Vitae	Unchanging friendship
Acacia, pink	Elegance
Acacia, yellow	Secret love
Acacia Rose	Friendship
Agrimony	Thankfulness
Almond, Flowering	Hope
Amaryllis	Splendid beauty, beautiful but timid
Anemone	Forsaken
Apple Blossom	Better things to come, good fortune
Arbor Vitae	Unchanging friendship
Arbutus, trailing	Welcome
Aster	Variety
Azalea	Temperance
Bachelor's Button	Single blessedness
Bells of Ireland	Good luck
Bluebell	Constancy, humility, gratitude
Buttercup	Riches, memories of childhood
Camellia	Excellence, perfect loveliness, gratitude
Camellia, white	Perfect loveliness
Canterbury Bells	Gratitude
Carnation	Distinction, fascination, pure and deep love

Flower	Meaning
Carnation, pink	Woman's love
Carnation, red	Alas, my poor heart
Carnation, yellow	Disdain
Carnation, white	Good luck gift
Chrysanthemum	A wonderful friend, cheerfulness in old age
Chrysanthemum, red	I love you, sharing
Chrysanthemum, white	Truth
Clover, four-leaf	Be mine
Clover, white	I promise
Coronilla	Success to you
Columbine	Folly
Columbine, purple	Resolved to win
Columbine, red	Anxious and trembling
Crocus	Abuse not
Daffodil	Regard, unrequited love
Dahlia	Dignity and elegance
Daisy	Innocence
Daisy, garden	I share your feelings
Daisy, single field	I will be thinking of you
Daisy, white	Purity
Dandelion	Oracle, coquetry
Fern	Fascination, sincerity
Forget-me-not	True love
Foxglove	Insincerity, occupation
Fuchsia	Taste
Gardenia	Joy

Flower	Meaning
Geranium	True friend, stupidity, folly
Geranium, oak-leaved	True friendship, lady deigns to smile
Geranium, rose	I prefer you
Gorse	Endearing affection
Heather, white	Wishes will come true
Heliotrope	Devotion
Hepatica	Confidence
Holly	Foresight, good wishes
Honeysuckle	Generous affection, fidelity, devotion
Hyacinth	Loveliness, constancy, benevolence, sport, play
Hydrangea	Boastfulness
Iris	Warmth of affection, my compliments, your friendship means so much to me
Ivy	Fidelity, affection, matrimony, wedded love
Japonica	Loveliness
Jasmine	Grace, elegance, amiability
Jonquil	Desire for return of affection,
Larkspur	Levity, fickleness
Lavender	Distrust
Lemon Blossom	Fidelity in love
Lilac, purple	First emotions of love, regal unity
Lilac, white	Youthful innocence
Lily	Majesty
Lily, white	Purity and modesty
Lily, yellow	Gratitude

Flower	Meaning
Lily of the Valley	Happiness, return of happiness
Lily, Water	Purity of heart
Lupine	Dejection
Magnolia	Perseverance, dignity
Maidenhair	Discretion
Marigold	Sacred affection
Marigold, garden	Grief, chagrin
Mignonette	Your qualities surpass your charms
Mimosa	Secret love, sensitivity
Morning Glory	Coquetry, affection
Myrtle	Love, remembrance, love in absence
Narcissus	Egotism
Orange Blossom	Purity, festivities, virginity
Orchid	Rare beauty
Palm Leaves	Victory and success, immortality
Pansy, purple	You occupy my thoughts
Peach Blossom	Captive
Peony	Bashfulness
Periwinkle	Sweet memories
Pimpernel	Rendezvous, change
Poppy, red	Consolation
Poppy, scarlet	Extravagance, fantastic
Poppy, white	Rest, sleep, dream
Primrose	Modest worth, silent love
Phlox	Our hearts are united
Rose	Love
Rose, pink	Innocent love

Flower	Meaning
Rose, red	I love you
Rose, white	I am worthy of you, pure love
Rose, yellow	Friendship
Rosebud	Pure and lovely
Rosemary	Remembrance
Snapdragon	Presumption
Snowdrop	Hope, consolation, friend in adversity
Solidago	Success
Starwort, American	Welcome to a stranger
Stephanotis	You boast too much
Stock	Lasting beauty
Sunflower	False riches
Sunflower, dwarf	Your devout admirer
Sweet Pea	Delicate pleasure, lasting pleasure, a meeting
Sweet William	Gallantry
Thyme	Activity
Teasel	Misanthropy
Tuberose	Dangerous pleasure
Tulip	Fame, luck
Tulip, red	Declaration of love
Tulip, yellow	Hopeless love
Verbena	May you get your wish
Veronica	Fidelity
Violet	Faithfulness
Violet, blue	Constancy, modesty
Violet, white	Purity, candor, modesty

Flower	Meaning
Wisteria	Welcome fair stranger
Woodbine	Fraternal love
Wood Hyacinth	Constancy
Zinnia	I mourn your absence
Zinnia, magenta	Lasting affection
Zinnia, mixed	Thoughts (or in memory) of absent friends and remembrance, missing you

TREES ASSOCIATED WITH FAIRIES

ASH *(Fraxinus excelsior)* is one of the sacred trees in Wicca that is also connected with fairy lore. It is said that where this tree grows with the oak and the thorn, fairies can be seen and visited with.

In Norse mythology the god Odin is said to have hung from an ash tree in order to gain enlightenment. Speared in the side, his blood dripped upon the soil beneath him, forming the mystical symbols that we now call runes. In this tale the ash tree passes to Odin the ability to read the symbols. From the ash Odin also receives the gift of divination.

In ancient Aegean/Mediterranean mythology the goddess Nemesis carries an ash branch as a symbol of divine justice. Nemesis is also depicted in ancient art with an eight-spoke wheel symbolizing the solar year. The wheel is likewise the symbol of the Fates (particularly the spinning wheel), and therefore the ash is a symbol of Fate.

In Norse mythology the ash tree known as Yggdrasil is also known as the World Tree. It is the tree of the universe, of time and of life. Yggdrasil is tended by mythological beings known as Norns, who water it from the Life Fountain of Urd.

HAWTHORN *(Crataegus monogyna)* is the third magickal tree in the triad of fairy lore: oak, ash, and thorn. The hawthorn is associated with May Day, in honor of the sun god Belenus. His festival commenced on the first day that the hawthorn blossoms opened, and is now celebrated on May 1. In Ireland the hawthorn, or whitethorn, is sometimes called the fairy bush.

In ancient times, sprigs of hawthorn and hawthorn flowers were collected on May Day and taken home to banish evil. In Teutonic lore the hawthorn was a symbol of death and its wood was used for funeral pyres. In ancient Greece, wedding couples wore crowns made of hawthorn

blossoms while the wedding party carried torches of hawthorn wood. The Roman goddess Cardea, who presided over marriage and childbirth, was associated with the hawthorn in ancient Italy. Images of Cardea depict her with a bough of hawthorn.

The hawthorn tree was thought to protect the oak and ash, which were believed to be doorways into the fairy realm. The hawthorn prevented easy access through the oak and ash doorways, keeping the fairy realm hidden from human sight. In Celtic lore, the hawthorn was associated with Blodeuwedd, the wife of Lleu. She betrayed him and he was wounded with a spear, hence the association with the thorn. Sometimes Blodeuwedd is called the Queen of May. The goddess Cardea, in her aspect as Flora, is associated with May festivals in which she is also the Queen of May.

OAK *(Quercus petraea and Quercus robur)* is one of the most venerated trees since ancient times. To the Greeks and Romans the oak was sacred to Zeus/Jupiter, and was believed to speak oracle through the movement of its leaves. This associates the oracle with the wind and therefore with fairies who are creatures of air.

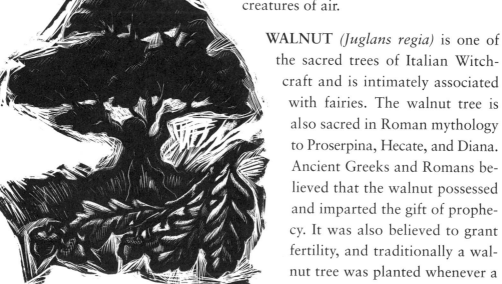

WALNUT *(Juglans regia)* is one of the sacred trees of Italian Witchcraft and is intimately associated with fairies. The walnut tree is also sacred in Roman mythology to Proserpina, Hecate, and Diana. Ancient Greeks and Romans believed that the walnut possessed and imparted the gift of prophecy. It was also believed to grant fertility, and traditionally a walnut tree was planted whenever a female was born to a family. When the daughter married the tree was cut and made into her marriage bed. In Italian folklore fairies sometimes dwell inside walnut shells and can be found in and around walnut trees. The "shell-game," where a pea is placed beneath one of three shells and then mixed around, is derived from a method of divination using walnut shells.

SACRED PLANTS ASSOCIATED WITH GODDESSES

Goddess	Sacred Plant
Aphrodite	Apple, cypress, daisy, myrtle, olive, orris
Aradia	Fennel, rue, vervain
Artemis	Cedar, daisy, date palm, hazel, myrtle, oak, silver fir, willow
Astarte	Alder, cypress, juniper, myrtle, pine
Bast	Catnip, vervain
Bellona	Belladonna
Brigit	Blackberry
Cailleach	Wheat
Cardea	Arbutus, fava bean, hawthorn
Ceres	Bay, leek, narcissus, pomegranate, poppy, wheat, willow
Cerridwen	Acorns, vervain
Cyble	Myrrh, oak, pine
Demeter	Barley, fava bean, myrrh, pennyroyal, pomegranate, poppy, rose, spelt grain, wheat
Diana:	Acacia, apple, beech, birch, dittany, fir, hazel, mugwort, mulberry, rue, willow, wormwood
Freya	Cowslip, daisy, maidenhair, myrrh, mistletoe, primrose
Hathor	Coriander, grape, myrtle, mandrake, rose, sycamore
Hecate	Aconite, cyclamen, cypress, date palm, garlic, henbane, mandrake, mint, onion, willow, yew
Hekat	Cypress
Hera	Apple, myrrh, orris, myrrh

Goddess	Sacred Plant
Hulda	Elder, flax, hellebore, rose
Irene	Olive
Iris	Iris, wormwood
Ishtar	Acacia, grains, juniper
Isis	Barley, fig, heather, iris, lotus, myrrh, palm, rose, wheat, wormwood
Juno	Ashpodel, crocus, fig, quince, mint
Minerva	Thistle, mulberry, olive.
Nepthys	Lily, myrrh
Nuit	Sycamore
Persephone	Grains, pomegranate, narcissus, willow
Rhea	Myrrh, oak
Venus	Anemone, apple, carnation, daisy, elder, heather, marjoram, myrtle, orchid, poppy, violet, vervain
Vesta	Oak

MAGICAL CORRESPONDENCES OF TREES

Goddess	Sacred Plant
Almond	Clairvoyance, divination, moon magick, wisdom
Apple	Healing, love, perpetual youth, prosperity
Ash	Protection
Apricot	Love
Aspen	Protection
Birch	Fertility, new beginnings, protection, purification
Cedar	Longevity, prosperity
Coconut	Chastity, healing, purity

Goddess	Sacred Plant
Cypress	Past-life workings, protection
Elder	Healing, prosperity, protection
Elm	Protection
Eucalyptus	Healing
Fig	Fertility, healing, sensuality
Hawthorn	Cleansing, love, protection
Hazel	Divination, protection, reconciliation
Juniper	Protection
Lemon	Chastity, divination, friendship, healing, wishing
Maple	Divination, love
Mulberry	Divination, knowledge, will power, wisdom
Oak	Healing, finances, longevity, strength
Olive	Fidelity, fruitfulness, peace, security
Orange	Love, marriage
Palm:	Strength
Peach	Divination, love
Pine	Fortune, fertility, health, prosperity, purification
Rowan	Protection, strength
Walnut	Divination, healing, oracle, protection
Willow	Enchantment, healing, moon magick, protection
Yew	Altered states of consciousness

5

SPELLS AND RECIPES

O do not tell the Priests of our Arts
For they would call it sin;
For we will be in the woods all night,
A-conjuring Summer in.

—*The Grimoire of Lady Sheba*

Spring rituals have long been associated with fertility, gain, and prosperity. The endless cycle of renewal suggested to humankind that something unseen was in control of the forces behind such cycles. From a desire to tap into this hidden power, or to persuade it to assist humankind, arose the creation of rituals and spells. Early magical reasoning held that in order to attract something, one needed to display an object that was similar in nature. Therefore certain plants, stones, and other natural objects were valued in magic because something in their shape, color, or property was suggestive of things desired by our ancestors.

In modern folk magic a green candle is said to help attract money. Eggs are believed to possess the magical power of fertility. Such things are very common elements employed in folk magic. Special charms and talismans can be added to strengthen one's belief while performing a ritual or casting a spell. Folk magic itself is a blend of employing natural objects, personal faith, and the powers of the mind toward manifesting a goal or desire.

SPELLS

In the following section are four types of spells that are popular with the modern practitioner of magick. When working magick it is important to also do the work on the physical plane.

A spell is designed to give your mundane efforts a boost. Spells are not intended to replace self-responsibility. Once you have put out the physical effort, then you can employ the following spells. Unless otherwise stated, perform these spells on the first day of the new moon.

MONEY DRAWING SPELL

3 green candles
1 aventurine stone
1 lodestone
   Patchouli incense
   Patchouli oil
   A small pouch containing cinnamon,
        peppermint, and comfrey

This spell should be worked when the waxing crescent of the moon can be seen in the night sky. Begin by anointing the candles with the patchouli oil. Then place them in holders, setting them to form a triangle surrounding the aventurine stone and the lodestone. Next anoint yourself on the solar plexus with patchouli oil. Light the candles and take three deep breaths through the closed herbal pouch. As you inhale, close your eyes and imagine a green sphere of energy pass into your solar plexus.

Now pick up the lodestone in your left hand and the aventurine stone in your right. Then speak this affirmation:

> *All obstacles are gone and I draw prosperity to*
> *myself. I attract gain and increase. I draw the abun-*
> *dance. To me comes now the money that is needed*
> *and to spare.*

Sit quietly in front of the candles and visualize yourself looking into your purse or wallet and having lots of cash. Next, see yourself writing checks to cover your bills and having a nice balance left in your checkbook.

Extinguish the candles and incense. Repeat the spell for three days in a row.

The accoutrements of a Money Drawing Spell.

SUCCESS SPELL

2   gold candles
1   red jasper stone
1   coin (any kind)
    A small pouch containing frankincense, cedar,
        and Solomon's seal
    Pennyroyal oil
    Sandalwood incense

When the moon is full, place the two gold candles in holders and set the red jasper stone and the coin in front of them. Center the incense behind the candles. Anoint the candles with pennyroyal oil and then light the candles and incense. Then take three deep breaths through the closed herbal pouch.

Next, pick up the coin and place it on your left palm. Turn the coin over three times, reciting the following for each turn of the coin:

> *Lady Moon, Queen of the Heavens*
> *see how I turn the coin as in days of old.*
> *Keep now the ancient promise*
> *that all who keep the turning of the wheel*
> *will prosper in all things.*

Pick up the stone in your right hand and relax for a few moments. Then visualize the successful outcome of your venture. See it clearly in your mind's eye exactly as you want it to occur.

Next anoint the stone and the coin with pennyroyal oil. Then pass each one through the incense smoke three times, and recite the following verse each time:

Here beneath the moon I see,
blessed be the spell times three,
success in all I do shall be,
and as my will, so mote it be!

Allow the candles and incense to burn out by themselves. Finish the spell by putting the stone and the coin in a small pouch. Keep it with you in your pocket or purse for seven days.

Triangular placement of candles for Success Spell.

LOVE ATTRACTING SPELL

2 green candle
1 red candle
1 rose quartz crystal
1 heart-shaped charm
Wisteria or frangipani incense
A bottle of your favorite perfume/cologne
A small pouch containing a pinch of vervain
and 3 rose petals

The purpose of this spell is to attract a person to you with whom you can have a loving relationship. It is not designed to attract a specific person that you desire. Spells that manipulate or compel other people to do as you will them to do are not considered ethical. This spell is for general attraction, a call to the Universe to send someone to you that will result in a mutually loving relationship.

Arrange the candles so that they form a triangle. The triangle needs to be wide enough to place the crystal and the heart charm in the open center of the triangle.

Light the candles and incense. Pick up the sealed herbal pouch and inhale through it three times.

Pick up the rose quartz in your right hand and the heart charm in your left. Stretch out your arms so that your body forms a "T" posture. Then speak the following:

> *I call out now to the four quarters,*
> *bring to me upon the mist of magick*
> *the one with whom my heart will sing.*
> *Hear me, hear my cry:*

> *I call upon the spirits of air to carry her/him to me.*
> *I call upon the spirits of water to let love flow*
>   *within us.*
> *I call upon the spirits of fire to ignite our passion*
> *I call upon the spirits of earth to bind us together.*

Immediately after saying the last line, cross your arms over your chest, forming an "X" pattern, and take three slow, deep breaths. Then place the heart charm and quartz piece on the herbal bag.

Pick up the perfume/cologne bottle, pass it through the incense three times, and then spray some perfume/cologne on your heart area. Next, speak the following:

> *By the spirits of earth, air, fire, and water,*
> *may the emanation of this scent*
> *fill my aura and draw to me*
> *a loving partner of mind, spirit, and body.*
> *with harm to none, so mote it be.*

Allow the candles and incense to burn out on their own. Put the charm and the quartz piece into the herbal bag and carry it with you in your purse or pocket for one full cycle of the moon. When you are out in social settings put on some of your perfume or cologne. Do not keep thinking on the spell, but instead let it work on its own.

SERENITY SPELL

1 sage smudge bundle
1 blue candle
1 pink candle
  Sandalwood oil
  Sandalwood incense
1 amethyst stone
  A small pouch containing a pinch each
    of lilac, sage, and chamomile

Ideally this spell should be performed while taking a nice relaxing bath to enhance its effectiveness. Begin by lighting the smudge stick and pass the smoke around you from head to toe. Next fill the tub with water. Then take the blue and pink candles and anoint them with the sandalwood oil. Place the candles on the edge of the bathtub so that you will be looking directly at them. Set the amethyst stone on the side edge of the tub. Light the incense and set it away from the bathtub. When you are ready, turn out any lights so that only the candles glow.

Get into the tub and settle down into the water. After a few moments take the amethyst stone in your hand and close your eyes. Take three deep breaths, inhaling and exhaling slowly. Mentally identify the things that are causing you stress, one situation at a time. Do not dwell on each one, but simply identify them. Once identified, take a deep breath, inhaling through the closed herbal pouch, exhaling out upon the amethyst stone. As you do so, feel that you are literally blowing the negative emotional energy away, out of your body. Then dip the stone into the water and briskly pass the stone through the water as though you were rinsing something off it, which indeed you are.

When you have completed the process, immediately leave the bathtub, initiate draining the tub, and then dry yourself off with a towel. At this point take the candles and incense to a quiet place where you can either sit or lie down comfortably. Anoint yourself with the sandalwood oil. Gaze upon the burning candles a few moments, and then make this affirmation:

> *I claim this time of peace as my own and allow nothing else to enter into this moment. All is in harmony, my spirit embraces tranquility. Nothing but good shall come to me, nothing but good shall come from me.*

If possible allow the candles to go out on their own. Spend a few moments reflecting upon the things that are good in your life, and the people whom you love and who love you. Put the stone into the herbal bag and carry in your purse or pocket for seven days.

DIVINATION

With the changing of seasons and the approach of summer, works of divination are useful to gain new perspectives. In ancient times dark pools of liquid were used to divine the future. This represented the look within, the assessment of the past, and its gift to the future. The old term for this type of divination is known as "scrying." Scrying is a very ancient technique common among shamanistic traditions. Divination itself is the ability to discern patterns that are forming, moving toward manifestation. What you "see" is actually what is likely to occur if nothing changes the divinatory images one perceives.

The use of a scrying bowl is one of the traditional methods of fortune-telling. This very basic method employs a dark liquid formula. Pour some bottled water into a medium-sized bowl such as a soup bowl. Add a few drops of blue or green food coloring to the water, enough to ensure that the liquid is dark and obscures the bottom of the bowl. At this point you should have a dark, reflective surface to gaze into. Place two candles as your source of light, making sure that the light does not reflect upon the liquid. Setting them a foot or two in front of you, one candle off to each side, should work.

Next, perform a series of hand passes over the liquid in the bowl, slowly and deliberately. In the magickal arts, the right hand generates an electrical charge and the left hand a magnetic charge. Left-handed passes attract and draw images, forming them in the dark liquid. Right-handed passes will strengthen the images appearing there, and focus them more clearly.

A dark, reflective surface is best for scrying.

Begin scrying by making left-handed passes over the bowl, in a clockwise circle, just a few inches above the water (palms open and facing down). Stop and gaze into the dark liquid, not at its surface but deep into the bowl. Usually several repeated passes of the hands are required during the scrying process. Alternate between the left hand and the right hand. This requires patience, and time. Use your intuition as you sit before the bowl. Make sure the area is quiet and there are no distractions.

With practice, images will begin to form within the liquid. Sometimes they will be symbolic or suggestive images. At other times they may form as faces, objects, or places you are already familiar with. It is important to simply allow the images to form. Do not rush them, or become anxious when they begin to appear. Try to remain calm and receptive. Watch the images until they fade away. At first, interpreting the meaning of what you see is like trying to find meaning within a dream, but, with time, you will begin to understand the symbols, their meaning, and the importance of their appearance.

THE SCRYING GLASS

The scrying glass is a dark concave surface of reflective material. One can easily be constructed by using the curved glass face of a clock and painting the convex side with glossy black paint. Once the paint has thoroughly dried, bath the mirror in an herbal brew of rosemary, fennel, rue, vervain, ivy, and walnut leaves (or bark). If you want to be truly traditional, pour some sea foam into the mixture.

To charge the glass, take a deep breath and then slowly exhale outward upon the potion. Repeat this three times. Remove the mirror from the potion and dry it off thoroughly. Prop the mirror up vertically, supported by two sturdy books or book ends to hold it in place. Hold your right hand out in front of you so that your palm is facing the convex side of the mirror. Then place the left palm facing the concave side, about three inches away from the glass surface. You are now ready to magnetize the mirror.

With the left hand begin making a circular clockwise motion across the surface of the mirror. Do this for a few minutes and then repeat this on the convex side of the mirror with the right hand. The opposite hand is always held still while the moving hand circulates. To use the scrying glass simply employ the same techniques as described for the divination bowl.

RECIPES FOR CELEBRATING MAY

Food is a magickal thing. The tools that harvest the raw materials and the items that cook the meal are all associated with ritual lore. Among the earliest tools were the cauldron and the hearth. The fire that burned in the hearth was a spirit, and the chimney connected the earth and the sky, drawing down the blessings of the divine and offering up the scent of food in a way of thanksgiving. Here in the hearth the fire could be evoked in order to initiate the process that would join the elements together to manifest a meal. Eating and sitting before the fire became a social event. It was a time to put aside the work of the day and join together as family and friends.

Most of the customary recipes associated with a season are steeped in cultural expression and ancient traditions. Planting and harvesting laid the foundation for many customs and traditions. Meals to celebrate the hard work of farming were made from what grew in season. For our ancestors, planting seeds involved breaking the soil and clearing the land with primitive tools by today's standards. In the past it took thirty people working for four days to bring in the harvest. The accomplishment of such a task was celebrated with a festive meal. Today a tractor can perform the same task in a single day, something that calls for a less spectacular celebration. Sadly the old traditions have all but disappeared now, but we can recapture them.

Few celebrations of May would be complete without the presence of May wine. May wine is made from the earliest harvest of grapes. It is very popular among modern celebrants of Beltane and is also used as an offering of "first fruits" to the Goddess and God. It is easily purchased at most stores that carry even a fair selection of wine. However, there is a quick and easy way to create a suitable May wine if none can be found to purchase.

A Quick May Wine

Obtain a bottle of white table wine (not a Chardonnay) and pour the contents into a larger glass container that has a lid. Next take a half-dozen to a dozen bruised fresh strawberries and slice them. Then add a few sweet woodruff leaves and the berries to the wine and chill for several hours to allow the flavors to develop.

BLESSING FOR MAY WINE

Place the wine in the center of a wreath of flowers. Hold your hands over the wine, palms down, and recite the blessing:

Blessings be upon this wine, which is the essence of the secret of transformation. The blood of life flows again back into Nature and summer approaches with the promise of fullness. May all who drink this wine be filled to the brim with all that is good in life.

MAKING A MAY CUP

The May cup is an English tradition in which one offers the cup to guests and travelers during the May Day celebrations. The May Cup is easily prepared (although it takes about two hours to settle) and tastes delicious.

- 4 glasses of white wine
- 8 glasses of cider
- 1 glass of brandy
- 1 orange, sliced
- ½ ounce ladies' bedstraw *(Galium verum)*

Mix the white wine, cider, and brandy together. Then add the orange slices and ladies' bedstraw. Leave the mixture in a cool place to settle for two hours, and then filter the liquid into a jug. Serve in glasses.

The traditional main dish of a May celebration is fish, lamb, or pork. For the vegetarian mushrooms with pasta (seasoned with onion, celery, pepperocini, and basil) is a good alternative.

As part of the May celebration you may wish to include some special treats for the celebrants. In addition to the main feast a dessert is always welcome. In keeping with the traditions of May, any of the following will do nicely.

BACCHUS PUDDING

4	eggs
1¼	cups confectioner's sugar
2½	cups sweet white wine (such as Riesling)
½	cinnamon stick
3	whole cloves

Preheat oven to 300°F.

Beat eggs well, then set aside until foam subsides. Boil the sugar and wine together with the cinnamon and cloves for about 5 minutes. Set the mixture aside to cool. Remove the cinnamon stick and cloves. Press the beaten eggs through a strainer to eliminate the rest of the foam and any impurities. Blend both mixtures together.

Pour the mixture into custard cups and set them in a baking pan. Fill the pan with boiling water to a level 1 inch up the sides of the cups. Bake for 55 minutes, until the puddings have set and a skewer comes out almost completely clean.

CUSTARD (MICROWAVE RECIPE)

1	cup milk
4	eggs
2	tablespoons honey or sugar

Beat together until thoroughly blended. Divide into 3 or 4 small microwave containers.

Cook at 30% power in 600–700 watt oven or at 50% power in 500–600 watt oven (1 custard 6–7 min., 2 custards 9–11 min., 3 custards 12–15 min., 4 custards 15–22 min.). Turn as necessary for even cooking. Custards are done when a knife inserted near the center comes out clean. Let custard stand 5 minutes before serving. Yield: 2 cups.

PORRIDGE

Porridge was one of the main ways of eating oats in days gone by. There is a lot of mystique about making porridge and lots of traditions associated with cooking and eating it. Stirring the porridge should always be clockwise (even though going in different directions probably mixes it more efficiently). Porridge used to be served with separate bowls of double cream. A spoonful of porridge (in a horn spoon) was dipped into a communal bowl of cream before eating. Tradition dictates that porridge is eaten standing up. Porridge used to be poured into a "porridge drawer." Once it had cooled, it could be cut up into slices, which were easier to carry than brittle oatcakes. The important thing is to obtain good quality medium-ground oats (rather than rolled oats), and to keep stirring it to avoid solid lumps.

    1   pint (half-liter) water, or use half water and half milk
    2½ ounces (2½ rounded tablespoons) medium-ground oats
        Pinch of salt

Bring the water (or water and milk) to a good rolling boil, preferably in a nonstick pan. Slowly pour the oatmeal into the boiling liquid, stirring vigorously with a wooden spoon all the time. Keep stirring until it has returned to the boil again, reduce the heat, cover the pan, and simmer very gently for 15 minutes, stirring frequently. Add the salt at this point and simmer and stir for a further 5–10 minutes (time depends on the quality of the oats). It should have a thick but pourable consistency. Porridge is traditionally served hot in wooden bowls. Yield: 2 servings.

MAY WREATH CAKE

¾ cup unbleached all-purpose flour
1 teaspoon sea salt
¾ cup sugar
1 teaspoon cinnamon
2 tablespoons baking powder
½ teaspoon baking soda
3 tablespoons olive oil
6 tablespoons vegetable oil
3 lemons
3 eggs
4 tablespoons rum
3 tablespoons milk
1½ tablespoons vanilla extract
½ teaspoon lemon extract

Preheat oven to 375°F.

In a large bowl mix the flour, salt, sugar, cinnamon, baking powder, and baking soda. Add the oils and mix with a wooden spoon or with the paddle of an electric mixer until crumbly. Grate the zest of the lemons directly over the mixture. Beat the eggs, rum, milk, and vanilla and lemon extracts together. Add this to the dry ingredients and stir until completely incorporated.

Shape the dough into a ball. Set it in a round baking pan (9½ to 10-inch round) lined with parchment paper, and using your hands, make a hole in the center. Gradually stretch the dough from the center, increasing the size of the hole to about 6 inches wide. The hole will close up somewhat during baking. Makes one round cake:

Bake at 375°F, until a tester comes out clean, about 45 minutes.

Icing for May Wreath Cake:

2   egg whites
2   tablespoons sugar
   Colored sprinkles

Just before the cake is finished baking, beat the egg whites briskly until they form soft peaks. Add the sugar and beat until glossy. Remove the cake from the oven, spread the icing over the top, then shower with colored sprinkles, and return to the oven for 5 minutes, or until icing is lightly browned.

MAY SERPENT CAKE

¾   cup of sugar
½   teaspoon of ground cloves
1½ teaspoons ground nutmeg
   Grated zest of 1 orange
1   teaspoon baking soda
¾   teaspoon salt
4½ cups plus 2 tablespoons unbleached all-purpose flour
½   cup unsalted butter
¾   cup plus 3 tablespoons honey, boiling
½   cup strong-brewed espresso coffee
1   egg
⅓   cup amaretto or rum
⅓   cup wild cherry or raspberry jam
   Coffee beans and candied orange peel for garnish

Preheat oven to 400°F.

Mix the sugar, spices, orange zest, baking soda, and salt into the flour. Cut in the butter with a pastry blender until it is the size of small pebbles. Pour in the boiling honey, coffee, and liqueur, and mix until smooth. Let cool and then turn out onto a floured surface.

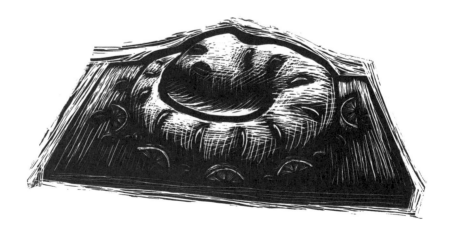

Divide the dough in half. Roll the first half into an 18-inch long cylinder. Make a deep trough down the center and carefully spoon half the jam in it. Pull the edges of the dough out and over the jam and pinch firmly all along the length to seal the jam firmly inside. Roll the log over and carefully place it, seam side down, on a baking sheet lined with parchment paper. Be sure that the smooth side is up. Bend the dough carefully into a circle and fashion the snake's head at one end, making a triangle shape. Taper the other end to make the tail of the snake's body. Firmly set in two coffee beans for the snake's eyes. Repeat for second cake. Bake the cakes at 400°F for about 30 minutes. Makes two cakes.

OAT CAKES (BANNOCKS)

Oatcakes are an old tradition and were cooked on a griddle, over an open fire. Today a heavy frying pan is more commonly used.

Ingredients:

    4   ounces (125 grams) medium oatmeal
        Pinch of salt
    2   pinches of baking soda
    2   teaspoons melted fat (bacon fat is traditional)
    ¾   tablespoon hot water
        Additional oatmeal for kneading

Mix the oatmeal, salt, and soda in a bowl, then pour the melted fat into the center of the mixture. Stir well, using a porridge stick if you have one, and add enough water to make a stiff paste. Cover the work surface with oatmeal and turn the mixture onto this. Work quickly as the paste is difficult to work if it cools. Divide dough into two parts, roll one half into a ball and knead, with hands covered in oatmeal to keep from sticking. Roll out to about one-quarter inch thick. Put a plate that is slightly smaller than the size of your pan over the flattened mixture and cut around it to make a circular oatcake. Cut into quarters and place in a heated pan that has been lightly greased. Cook for about 3 minutes, until the edges curl slightly, turn, and cook the other side. Prepare another oatcake while the first is cooking.

An alternative method of cooking is to bake the cakes in an oven at 375°F/190°C for about 30 minutes, or until brown at the edges. The quantities above will be enough for two bannocks about the size of a dessert plate. If you want more, do them in batches rather than making larger quantities of mixture. Store in a tin and reheat in a moderate oven before serving.

THE FERTILE MONTH OF MAY

May, as the herald of the coming season of summer, when crops grow to fullness, is often associated with fertility. In this section various herbs traditionally believed efficacious for pregnancy and the female reproductive system are discussed. The herbs and remedies listed here are traditional folk remedies, included here for their historical interest. *Do not use any of the following remedies without first consulting a doctor to ensure that these herbs are safe for you as an individual.*

To Increase Chances of Pregnancy

- To increase fertility, add small amounts of powdered cayenne to food or herbal tea.

- Chicory leaves or flowers will also increase a woman's fertility.

- Red clover will restore alkaline balance to the body and thereby possibly boost fertility.

- Licorice stimulates production of female hormones.

- Raspberry leaf is excellent while trying to get pregnant, but should be discontinued once conception occurs, until the last two months of pregnancy when it is safe to drink raspberry tea again. The tea also helps ease labor. Use one teaspoon of dried herb to one cup of boiling water.

For Morning Sickness

- Chamomile flower heads are excellent brewed as a tea for morning sickness.

- Ginger root is also good for relieving nausea. Use one teaspoon to two cups of water.

- Marjoram is good for morning sickness and nausea. Use one heaping teaspoon to two cups of water.

- Peppermint will also help with nausea and an upset stomach.

- A tea made of two parts meadowsweet, one part black horehound, and one part chamomile may be taken three times a day.

To Calm a Threatened Miscarriage

- Black currant berries can be eaten to prevent a threatened miscarriage.

- Several hollyhock leaves added to a heated wine is also good.

- Another excellent herb is rosemary. Add a tablespoon of fresh leaves (dried, half a tablespoon) to boiling water, steep for five minutes, and then strain before drinking.

- Drink a tea (three times a day) made of two parts blue cohosh (*Caulophyllum thalictriodes*), two parts false unicorn root (*Chamaelirium luteum*), and one part cramp bark (*Viburnum opulus*).

- Drink hollyhock tea (use a handful of leaves to one pint of boiling water, simmer ten minutes, strain, and add a pinch each of ginger and cinnamon).

- Drink rosemary tea, using one tablespoon of fresh leaves (half-tablespoon dried) to a cup of boiling water; steep ten minutes and strain.

NURSING

- To promote milk flow: Avoid parsley and sage because they can slow down early production of milk. Drink several cups a day of the following tea:

  Bruise half a teaspoon of caraway seeds, one teaspoon of dill seeds and two tablespoons of fennel leaves. Add to boiling water. Let steep for five minutes and then strain the liquid.

- These herbal teas are also useful in producing breast milk:

Borage	Vervain
Fenugreek	Watercress
Rosemary	Woodruff

- To decrease the flow of milk: Add large amounts of parsley to your diet and drink parsley tea and/or parsley soup to gradually decrease milk flow. Sage tea (especially red sage) is good for drying up the milk supply during the weaning process.

- For nipple leaking: Wet a cloth (or cotton ball) with witch hazel extract and apply to nipples.

- For sore nipples: Apply raw, scraped carrots directly to raw nipples. A poultice of comfrey root or leaf will heal sore or chapped nipples. Yarrow as a tea or a poultice is also good.

HERBAL TREATMENT RELATED TO A WOMAN'S BODY

- Uterine tonics have a specifically toning and strengthening action upon the whole system, both on the tissue of the organs and on their functioning. Remedies such as black cohosh, blue cohosh, chaste tree, false unicorn root, life root, motherwort, raspberry, and squaw vine are used as healers in a holistic sense.

TO STIMULATE AND BALANCE MENSTRUAL FLOW

- Tea made from any of the following:

Angelica	Life Root
Basil	Marigold (calendula)
Blue Cohosh	Motherwort
Dill	Parsley
Elecampane	Pennyroyal
False Unicorn Root	Rue
Fennel	Southernwood
Ginger	Squaw Vine
Lemon balm	Yarrow
Licorice	

TO EASE A HEAVY MENSTRUAL FLOW

- Add a few grains of cayenne pepper to an herbal tea, three times a day.

- Drink red raspberry tea three times a day.

- Eat lentil soup.

- Drink shepherd's purse tea, two cups three times a day (one handful of dried leaves to a pint of boiling water.

- Drink thyme tea, one cup in the morning and one cup at night.

FOR PAINFUL PERIODS

- Drink peppermint tea to relieve cramps and menstrual headaches.

- Drink catnip tea (one teaspoon of flowers to a cup of boiling water).

- Drink a cup of ginger tea (one teaspoon of grated root to one cup of boiling water).

HORMONAL NORMALIZERS

- The following group of herbs are indicated for endocrine treatment:

Burdock	Rue
Cleavers	Sarsaparilla
Dandelion	Violet Leaves
Echinacea	Wormwood
Golden Seal	Yarrow
Mugwort	Yellow Dock
Red Clover	

A MAY RITUAL

May, clad in cloth of gold,
    Cometh this way;
The fluting of the blackbirds
    Heralds the day.

—Attributed to Finn himself
Translated by Dal Riadh Celtic Trust

For most modern celebrants the rites of May, known as Beltane, mark the transition from winter to summer. In ancient Celtic religion winter and summer were the two halves of the Celtic year. Bonfires were lighted to encourage the return of warmth to the land. The name for May comes from the Latin root *mag*, which means to grow. This is also the root for the goddess name Maia, after whom the month is named. In ancient Rome, on May 1, a pregnant sow was sacrificed to Maia. This was the same sacrifice made to *Terra Mater* (Mother Earth), thereby closely identifying the two goddesses.

Deities are generally connected to May through myths that are associated with the May rite of Beltane. This serves to help us relate to the energies of the season as personification; in other words the forces of May become gods and goddesses in story form. In modern Wicca many traditions associate May with myths of the return of the Goddess from the Underworld. This, of course, is the classic tale of Persephone and Hades.

In ancient Rome, offerings were made on May Day to Lare spirits, who the Roman writer Ovid calls the "night watchmen." Lare are protectors of home, hearth, and lineage in archaic Roman religion. Altars were placed before small towers that were erected at the crossroads to honor the Lare.

Setting an altar to acknowledge and honor the May season is effective. The altar is a sign of your devotion and is a focal point for the mind and spirit during a ritual. Creating a sacred space to encompass the altar supports and amplifies the energy you bring to your ritual. Decorating the altar with flowers, statuary, and other items helps to create an atmosphere of celebration and devotion.

THE ALTAR

The use of an altar dates back to times of antiquity. Altars have been used in almost every culture in the world. Essentially the altar is a focal point, a point within the sacred space of a ritual circle where one can approach his or her own understanding of deity. By custom, an altar is oriented to the viewer so that he or she faces a particular quarter when attending the altar. In some traditions the altar is oriented to the East. At this quarter both the sun and moon rise, and many cultures have honored this direction as the source of enlightenment. In other traditions the altar faces North, the customary quarter of divine power among the ancient Etruscan and Celtic peoples.

Altars are constructed from various materials such as wood or stone. In ancient times large flat rocks were used as altars, as were tree stumps. Some rocks were large enough for a woman to recline upon, serving symbolically as the living altar of the Goddess Herself. Modern altars appear in many different shapes and sizes. Some are round, symbolizing the cycles of Nature. Other altars are rectangular and symbolize the Underworld and Overworld supported by the columns of light and darkness. In some Traditions the altar is cubical, representing the four elements of creation united in harmony.

Whatever your choice in an altar design, it should be pleasing to your personal taste in design and imagery. Carefully select any deity images you wish to place upon your altar to reflect the theme of May or spring. Other ritual decorations used upon the altar should also be reflective of the season. The altar is the meeting place between the mundane and the divine; it is sacred space and should reflect your devotion and veneration.

PREPARATION OF AN ALTAR

Setting up the altar is an important part of any ritual. It should be performed with focus and concentration upon the inner meanings as each item is placed on the altar, because you are creating your own universe as you lay out the altar within the sacred space you design. Everything you create here establishes your own separate reality. In a magickal sense your altar also serves as the "battery" for the ritual work. A well-established altar will serve as a catalyst to the magickal states of consciousness necessary for effective ritual work.

The May altar will feature Goddess and God statues as well as candles, and will be decorated with flowers of the season.

Since the altar is an important part of sacred space, before dedicating it to your ritual work, sprinkle it with purified water containing three pinches of salt. Pass the smoke of some burning incense, such as sandalwood or frangipani, over the altar. As you do so, speak your intent, declaring why you have erected the altar, and dedicate it to the May season and to the deity forms you call upon. For a general alignment you can simply use the terms "May Queen" and "May King," instead of the specific names of a goddess or god.

When you are ready to work with the altar, spread a black cloth over it to symbolize the darkness of "procreation" from which all things manifest. Over this place a colored altar cloth to symbolize May or spring. A green altar cloth is ideal. Then set a candle representing the Goddess at the upper left section of the altar, and another at the upper right section to symbolize the God. Statues of the Goddess and God may be placed next to the assigned candle accordingly. This symbolizes the presence of divinity overseeing the process of creation reflected in your altar setup as you continue to lay out the altar items. A full altar setup typically includes an incense burner, candle snuffer, container of purified water, ritual bell, and decorations associated with the season of the year. These are all arranged as is pleasing to your eye. May/spring altars are best adorned with flowers.

PREPARATION OF THE RITUAL CIRCLE

To create a sacred space in which to celebrate May, mark out a work area by forming a ritual circle on the ground. You can physically mark the circle by laying a ring of individual flowers on the ground. If this is not practical, then you can use a rope, stones, or even a chalk line. Once the circle is marked, place a small candle inside the circle at each of the North, East, South, and West quarters. Next perform the following steps:

1. Purify the ritual area by sprinkling salted water around the outline of the circle.

2. Set up the altar as previously described, using two green candles for the god and goddess position. Include another green candle and set it directly center on the altar. When you are ready to begin the ritual, light the center candle, then take a wand or blade and trace a triangle in the air over the altar and recite:

> *I acknowledge and align with the forces of this May*
> *season. I am in Nature and Nature is within me. As*
> *the season grows to fullness from this day forward,*
> *so too do all my endeavors grow into a rich harvest*
> *to come.*

3. Light the altar candles. Trace another triangle in the air over the altar and recite:

> *Beautiful goddess of this May season, majestic God*
> *of this May season, I ask for your blessings upon*
> *this sacred space that I establish in your honor.*

4. Conjure the elementals to assist in the construction of the ritual circle: face each of the four quarters (beginning North, then East, etc.) one at a time as you ring the bell three times. Recite the following to each quarter after ringing the bell:

> *I call out into the mist of Hidden Realms, and con-*
> *jure you spirits of Earth and Air and Fire and Water.*
> *Gather now at this sacred circle, and grant me*
> *union with your powers.*

5. Pick up your ritual blade and, beginning at the North, tread the circle clockwise. Point your blade down at the ground and imagine energy flowing out through your arm (like a hose) and down through the

blade. You are laying out a circle of light along the edge of the circle as you walk. Visualize a blue liquid flame pouring out through the blade into the circle's rim as you tread the circle, and recite as you go:

> *In the names of the God and Goddess,*
> *and by the spirits of Old,*
> *I conjure this circle of power:*
> *become a sphere of protection,*
> *a vessel to contain the power*
> *that shall be raised within,*
> *wherefore do I charge you,*
> *and empower you.*

6. Return to the altar and pick up the center green candle. Beginning North and moving clockwise, light each quarter candle with this candle flame. As you light each candle ask that the elemental watch over and protect the circle. For example, at the North say "Spirits of Earth, watch and protect this sacred circle" (North = Earth, East = Air, South = Fire, and West = Water).

7. Rap your wand three times on the altar and declare out loud that the circle is cast.

SOLITARY MAY
CELEBRATION RITUAL

A small crown of flowers
A small candle
A fresh flower
A Goddess statue
Ritual sword

1. Create a sacred space/cast a circle as previously prescribed.

2. Recite from the altar:

> *At this joyous time I welcome the return of the Goddess, the Queen of May. With her coming, flowers bloom and life is renewed upon the earth.*

3. Turn to the South quarter, and recite:

> *Season unto season, year unto year, all cycles pass one into the other. The Goddesses has returned to Her Hidden Children of Time. The Queen of May ever bestows love and peace, fullness and the promise of renewal.*

Place the crown of flowers in front of the Goddess statue.

4. Hold the sword up in front of the Goddess statue and say:

> *My lady, all power is given to You, for this is so ordained. And with love there is submission to Your ways, and reign is given over into Your hands.*

5. Recite the Charge of Aradia:

> *Whenever there is need of anything, once in the month when the moon is full, then shall due worship be given to She who is Queen of all.*
>
> *Here inside a circle, secrets that are as yet unknown shall be revealed. And the mind must be free and also the spirit. For this is the essence of spirit, and the knowledge of joy.*
>
> *Truth to one's beliefs is the keeper of the Ways, holding true despite all obstacles. For the Ways are the key to the mysteries and to the cycle of rebirth, which opens the way to the Womb of Enlightenment.*
>
> *In life does the Queen reveal the knowledge of spirit. And from death does the Queen deliver one to peace.*
>
> *It is right to give offerings to She who is our mother. For She is the beauty of the Green Wood, and the light of the moon among the stars, and the mystery which gives life, and draws one to Her name.*
>
> *Her worship is within the heart, and all acts of love and pleasure are rituals to the Goddess. But to seek her, desire is not enough until the secret is realized. Because if what one seeks is not found within, one will never find it from without. For she has been within the path you first entered, and she is that which awaits at the journey's end.*

6. Turn to the East quarter and recite:

> *Hail and adoration to the Lady of May.*
> *You who are the Great Moon Goddess,*
> *Queen of Heaven, Lady of the Earth,*
> *I welcome You, and rejoice in Your presence.*

A simple altar setting for a Solitary May Celebration Ritual.

Place a fresh flower at the East quarter and say:

Blessed be all in the name of the Goddess.

7. Then take a chalice of wine, whisper the name (or title) of the Goddess upon the surface of the wine, and then drink. By this act She passes into your inner self.

8. Ritual celebration continues with a small celebratory meal of cakes and wine.

After completing any ritual you will need to dissolve/banish the circle.

BANISHING A CAST CIRCLE (The circle must be dissolved when the ritual is completed):

1. Beginning at the North quarter, ring the bell three times, salute, and recite:

> *Hear me Old Ones,*
> *I honor You for Your attendance*
> *and bid You now depart to your secret Realms.*
> *With love I say now; Peace and farewell!*

2. Repeat the above action at each of the quarters (moving West, South, East, and North again).

3. Beginning at the North, point your ritual blade down toward the circle and walk counterclockwise, mentally drawing the blue light back up from the circle perimeter, into the blade.

After returning to the North quarter, go before the altar and point the tip of the ritual blade at the center of the altar. Visualize the power flowing back into the center candle. Recite the following invocation as you watch the candle flame:

I release and return the elements and powers back
to their source for the good of all and harm to none.
So mote it be!

Once you feel the energy has departed, dissolve the elements by extinguishing the quarter candles, giving thanks to the elemental spirits for their attendance, and then "snap" your fingers over the candle three times each. Begin this at the North and move counterclockwise.

4. Extinguish all the candles, giving thanks to the God and Goddess for their blessings. Declare that the circle is dissolved.

Group May Celebration Ritual

1. Create a sacred space as prescribed in this chapter.

2. Ritual begins with the High Priest addressing the attendants:

> *We gather at this joyous time and welcome the*
> *return of our Lady, and with her we rejoice as the*
> *season brings the blossom and the promise of much*
> *to come.*

3. At the North quarter, the High Priest invokes the Goddess upon the High Priestess, kneeling before her and touching her with the wand upon each breast and just below the navel, reciting:

> *Great Goddess of this May season,*
> *Thee I invoke,*
> *by stem, and leaf and bud.*

The Maiden then addresses the Grove:

> *By and by all things pass, season unto season, year*
> *unto year. Our Lady has come again to Her Hidden*
> *Children of Time. And our Goddess ever inclines*
> *to love and mirth, and guards and cherishes Her*
> *Hidden Children in Life. In Death She teaches the*
> *way to Her Communion, and even in this world She*
> *teaches them the mystery of the magic circle, which*
> *is placed between the worlds of men and of the*
> *gods. And our Lady descended, in times of old,*
> *into the Realm of Shadows. And the Lord of the*
> *Shadows was bewitched by Her Beauty. And He*
> *taught Her the mysteries of Death and Rebirth. And*
> *in love He bowed before Her and gave Her all of*
> *His Power.*

Attendants touch their chests at the heart, then touch fingertips to their lips, and then extend them toward the High Priestess. This is done much in the manner of "blowing a kiss."

4. High Priest kneels before the High Priestess and lays down his sword, saying:

> *My lady, I give all my power to You, for this is so*
> *ordained. And with love I submit to You, and I give*
> *my reign over to Your hands.*

5. High Priestess takes up the sword and gives the Charge of the Goddess:

Whenever you have need of anything, once in the month when the moon is full, then shall you come together at some deserted place, or where there are woods, and give worship to She who is Queen of All.

Come all together inside a circle, and secrets that are as yet unknown shall be revealed. And your mind must be free and also your spirit, and as a sign that you are truly free, you shall rejoice, and sing with music and love. For this is the essence of spirit, and a knowledge of joy.

Be true to your own beliefs, and keep to the Ways, beyond all obstacles. For ours is the key to the mysteries and the cycle of rebirth, which opens the way to the Womb of Enlightenment.

In life does the Queen of All reveal the knowledge of spirit. And from death does the Queen deliver you to peace. Give offerings all to She who is our mother. For She is the beauty of the green earth, and the white moon among the stars, and the mystery which gives life, and always calls us to come together in Her name. Let Her worship be the ways within your heart, for all acts of love and pleasure are like rituals to the Goddess. But to all who seek her, know that your seeking and yearning will reward

you not, until you realize the secret. Because if that
which you seek is not found within you, you will
never find it from without. For she has been with
you since you entered into the ways, and she is that
which awaits at your journey's end.

6. High Priestess moves to the East quarter, setting the sword before the altar as she goes, and stands as the Goddess. High Priest gives address:

> *Hail and adoration unto the Great Queen of the*
> *May. You who are the Great Star Goddess, Queen*
> *of Heaven, Lady of the earth, we welcome You, and*
> *rejoice in Your presence.*

All males and females will come forward and lay flowers before her.

7. The High Priest then takes a chalice of wine to the High Priestess. The High Priest then leads the attendants to the east quarter to receive the wine (essence of the Goddess) which they all drink of.

8. The High Priest will take a crown (of flowers) and place it upon the head of the High Priestess. They then embrace. All attendants next come forward and embrace the High Priestess also (one at a time). Each person will receive a candle (a token of the Life Force), which is lit from the Goddess candle, as High Priestess says:

> *Bear now the light of my season and walk always*
> *in balance. May the power of the forces of light be*
> *with you.*

Candles may be set aside for continuation of rite.

9. The attendants then form a circle along the ritual circle's perimeter

line, facing inward. Each person will then go around the circle, one at a time, embracing each member of the opposite gender, saying:

Blessed season, blessed be.

10. The ritual celebration continues with cakes and wine. Banish the circle as described for the solitary rite.

ARTS AND CRAFTS

I knot this garland
That love may bloom.
Love from the Earth!
Love from the Air!
Love from the Fire!
Love from the Water!
Garland of flowers,
Make love bloom.

—Scott Cunningham, *Spell Crafts*

The Beltane season is one of the most festive of the year. You can create both new and time-honored arts and crafts to celebrate Beltane. Perhaps you might even want to bring back some of the old May Day traditions such as leaving a small May basket of flowers on a neighbor's door or porch. The flowers can be selected according to their meanings in folklore, as noted in chapter 4.

The craft projects described in this chapter include a May Day wreath, a May garland, a Maypole table centerpiece, a May basket, and pentacle braids to enhance one's appearance at a May festival. Read over the instructions and note the supplies needed before trying to make any of the items.

MAY WREATH

Grapevine wreath
Variety of flowers
Greenery (ivy, rosemary, myrtle, etc.)
Decorative items (ribbons, figurine to set in
    wreath opening, raffi, etc.)
Scissors
Glue or hot glue gun

1. Assemble supplies: grapevine wreath, greenery, various flowers, moss, glue gun and glue sticks, scissors, and raffi.

2. The greenery goes on first. Weave, wrap, or tuck it into the grapevine. Glue it in strategic places if necessary. Ivy, myrtle, rosemary, and moss are just a few of the choices. Use fresh or dried. The moss tucks nicely into the grapevine weave.

3. Place a variety of flowers loosely around the greenery on the wreath before gluing them in place. If the flower has a stem, again it can be tucked into the grapevine and then glued at the base of the flower head. If the stems are brittle and break easily, just glue the flower head directly in place.

4. After all the flowers are in place you can add the little extra items that will make it unique. Use your imagination—ribbons, a fairy figure, beads, crystals, etc.

Materials needed for a May wreath.

*A completed May Day wreath, such as might decorate
the top of a Maypole (see pp. 10–11).*

MAY GARLAND

Sprigs of greenery (myrtle, rosemary, bay leaves, etc.)
Variety of fresh or dried flowers
Ribbons
Floral wire
Wire cutters
Scissors
Glue or hot glue gun and sticks

A single "backbone" that runs the full length of the garland is the secret to its structure. Heavy gauge wire for heavier materials such as evergreens is wise. Evergreens, herbs, fresh or dried flowers are just a few of the choices. Myrtle for May would be very appropriate as it is sacred to the fairies and is lightweight. Fresh flowers can be kept alive with floral water tubes.

The basic rule of construction is to start at one end and move toward the other, allowing each bundle of greenery to cover the means of attachment over the next one. Deciding how long you want the garland to be will determine how much material will be needed.

1. Assemble clumps of flowers, wrapping the stems together tightly with floral wire. Make as many as desired for every sprig or to be scattered throughout.

2. Wire flower clumps to sprigs of greenery, either on main stem area or to other stem parts (see illustration, p. 143).

4. Now use a continuous wire, unwinding the spool as you work (this is the spine). Start by overlapping one sprig onto another and wire together on the thickest stem parts. Try to obscure the wire wrap with greenery. Continue to wire together until the desired length is accomplished.

5. Here is the fun and finishing part—add ribbons (with bells or beads). Glue on buttons, beads, crystals, and seasonal decor. String the garland over the doorway, along the door jam, on the mantle, or wherever you desire (see below). Enjoy the vision.

Flower garlands such as this are one of summer's emblems.

MAYPOLE CENTERPIECE

18"	wood dowel or thin branch
6–9"	diameter flat round wooden plaque
	Small grapevine wreath, approximately 6–8" diameter, decorated on both sides.
1	yard each of red and white ribbon
	Scissors
	Drill and a ¼" drill bit (not pictured)
1	1¼" length flathead wood screw (adjust length to thickness of wood plaque as screw will need to extend through the plaque to secure the dowel on the other side)
	Hot glue gun and glue stick (or carpenter's glue)

1. Assemble your supplies: the dowel, round plaque, ribbons, glue gun and sticks, and the small grapevine wreath.

2. Drill pilot holes completely through the center of plaque and ½" deep into the bottom end of the dowel.

3. Cross the ribbons and glue on top end of the dowel.

4. Attach the dowel to the stand by screwing the screw through the plaque, and then into the bottom end of the dowel (figure A, p. 146).

5. Glue wreath on top of the dowel by melting a medium dab of glue on top of the crossed ribbons and on the bottom of the wreath, then join the wreath to the top of the dowel (figure B, p. 146). To make it more secure wait a few minutes and then glue around the edge of the wreath where it meets the dowel, filling in gaps.

6. Braid the ribbons—one color going left and under the other color, which is moving right. Braid about 2 inches down the dowel and tack

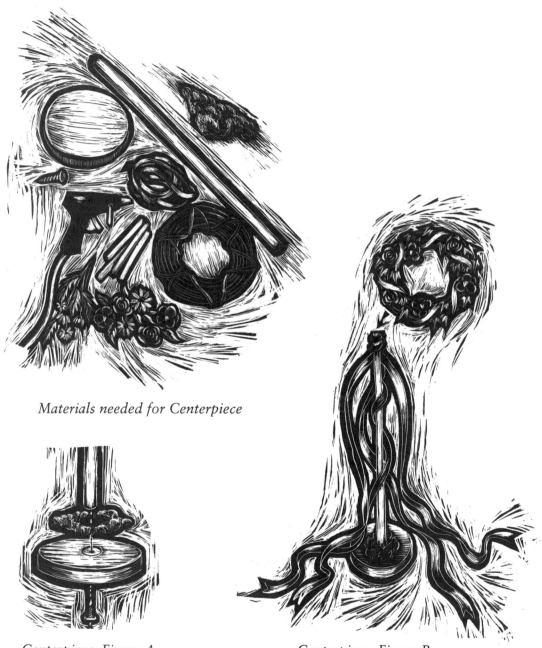

Materials needed for Centerpiece

Centerpiece, Figure A

Centerpiece, Figure B

to the dowel with hot glue to keep in place. When set, tack the ends of the ribbons to the edge of the wood plaque with hot glue.

7. You can also add a small figurine, a bird figure, or other symbolic items in the opening of the wreath.

MAY DAY CONE BASKET

Construction paper
Glue or tape

1. Out of bright colored construction paper cut a circle that is about 12 inches in diameter, then cut a triangle or wedge out of the circle, allowing for 1/2-inch overlap, as shown in figure A, p. 148. Roll the paper into a cone and glue or tape the two sides together (see figure C, p. 148).

2. Cut a strip of construction paper that is approximately 12 inches by 2 inches. Glue or tape it onto the top of your cone to make a handle (figure B, p. 148). Fill your cone basket with real or home-made flowers (p. 149) and hang it on a neighbor's or friend's doorknob in the early morning while everyone is asleep.

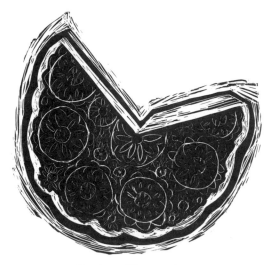

Basket, Figure A

Basket, Figure C

Basket, Figure B

A May basket filled with flowers carries a message to its recipient.

PENTACLE HAIR BRAIDS

1. Section off equal amounts of hair at the five points where the pentacle tips will be (see completed hairdo, figure C, for locations). Don't use all of the hair, just enough for the desired thickness of the pentacle.

2. Braid each section and then band ends of braid together with tiny rubber bands (figure A, below).

3. Form the braids into a pentacle design, and pin hair in place (figure B, p. 151). The remaining length of the braid should form the circle around the star pattern.

For remaining loose hair:

1. Braid hair (French braid) from top of head, around sides of pentacle, and band together at base of pentacle (figure C, p. 151). Then decorate with feathers, beads, ribbons, etc.

2. Or braid remaining hair (French braid) into crescent moons on either side of pentacle, then tuck tails back into braid.

Braids, Figure A

Braids, Figure B

Braids, Figure C

APPENDIX A:
MAY CELEBRATIONS
AROUND THE WORLD

Oak and May, / On This Day,
Will both Heed / Those in Need.
Goddess Bright, / God of Sun,
Bless your Children / 'Till our days are done.

—A general Beltane blessing chant

153

England

The festivities now associated with the celebration of May reached their height in England during the Middle Ages. They were heavily influenced by Italian forms of celebration dating back to the time of ancient Rome. On the first day of May, English villagers a rose at daybreak to wander the countryside gathering blossoming flowers and branches.

A towering tall Maypole was set up on the village green, which was typically the center of the village. The Maypole was made of the trunk of a tall tree, such as birch, and was decorated with bright flowers of the field. In celebration of the season, the villagers danced and sang around the Maypole, accompanied by the music of a piper. Often the morris dance was performed by dancers wearing colorful costumes upon which hung several small bells. The fairest maiden of the village was chosen to be the Queen of the May. In some regions of England a May King was also chosen. The Queen and King of May led the village dancers and ruled over the May Day festivities. During the Elizabethan period the king and queen were called Robin Hood and Maid Marian.

Maypoles were usually set up for the day in small towns and villages. In larger places, such as London, a permanent Maypole was erected. Eventually the Puritans spoke out against the Maypole and the revels of May as heathen practices. For a time they succeeded in eliminating the celebration of May, but the festivities returned within a few decades and continue in many English villages today.

An old English custom, still observed in some areas, involves a house-to-house visit by children, who bring flowers in exchange for pennies. Once the pennies are collected, the children toss them into a wishing well.

SWITZERLAND

In Switzerland a small May pine tree is often placed under a girl's window to encourage health, development, and fertility.

GERMANY

Here it is the custom for boys to secretly plant May trees in front of the windows of their sweethearts. This is said to ensure fidelity and the return of love.

GREECE

The acknowledgment of the May season begins with a custom linked to ancient omens. Greek children set out early in the morning to search for the first swallow of spring. When the bird is located, the children go from door to door, singing songs of spring. The neighbors in turn offer special treats to the children such as fruits, nuts, and cakes.

CZECHOSLOVAKIA

Like the German custom, at night boys place Maypoles by their sweethearts' windows.

FRANCE

Here the month of May is sacred to the Virgin Mary. Virginal young girls serve as May queens and lead processions in honor of the Virgin Mary, carrying a statue of the virgin crowned

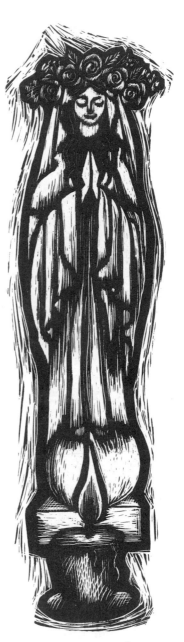

Virgin crowned as May queen.

with flowers. Cows appear in French May Day festivals, possibly as the remnant of a forgotten mother image or symbol of fertility and nurturing. Bundles of flowers are tied and draped around the cow's tail as they are led along in street parades. To touch one of the cows is believed to bring good luck, and everyone makes the attempt. An old custom that remains is to drink warm milk directly from the cow on May Day morning. This is said to bring good fortune throughout the coming year.

United States

Although May Day celebrations waned with the passing of the nineteenth century, a resurgence has been building. This seems to have been reborn on college campuses and at Renaissance fairs. Dancing and singing around a Maypole tied with colorful streamers or ribbons is no longer as uncommon as it was even twenty years. For May Day celebrations, a May Queen is chosen, but the King of May is not commonly chosen. An old custom also returning involves children constructing paper May baskets to hang on the doorknobs of relatives and friends. The children ring doorbells and run away, leaving their flowers as a surprise.

In Hawaii, May Day is called Lei Day. On this day a lei is given, with the giver putting it around the receiver's neck and accompanying it with the traditional kiss. Lei Day began in 1928 and is mixed with traditional Hawaiian celebrations complete with pageants, a Lei Queen, and her court.

ITALY

Although modern May festivals in Italy are associated with Mary and other saints, their history dates back to ancient Roman paganism. The people of ancient Rome honored Maia and Flora, the goddesses of flowers and springtime. Their statues were wreathed in garlands and carried in a procession of singers and dancers past a sacred, blossom-bedecked tree, the forerunner of the modern Maypole. Later, festivals of this kind spread to other lands conquered by the Romans. In many regions of modern Italy, boys often serenade their sweethearts on May Day.

BIBLIOGRAPHY

Alexander, Marc. *British Folklore.* London: Weidenfield and Nicholson Ltd., 1982.

Ankarloo, Bengt and Gustav Henningsen, editors. *Early Modern European Witchcraft.* Oxford: Clarendon Press, 1993

Arrowsmith, Nancy, and George Moorse. *A Field Guide to the Little People.* New York: Wallaby Books, 1977.

Bernstein, Frances. *Classical Living: Reconnecting with the Rituals of Ancient Rome.* New York: HarperCollins, 2000.

Briggs, K. M. *The Fairies in English Tradition and Literature.* London: Routledge & Kegan Paul, 1967.

Bunson, Matthew. *A Dictionary of the Roman Empire.* Oxford: Oxford University Press, 1991.

Burke, John. *Roman England.* London: Artus Books, 1983.

Burne, Charlotte Sophia. *The Handbook of Folklore: Traditional Beliefs, Practices, Customs, Stories, and Sayings.* London: Senate, 1995.

Collingwood, R. G. *Roman Britain.* New York: Barnes & Noble, by arrangement with Oxford University Press, 1994.

Cooper, J. C. *The Aquarian Dictionary of Festivals.* Wellingborough: Aquarian Press, 1990.

Day, Brian. *A Chronicle of Folk Customs.* London: Octopus Publishing Ltd., 1998.

Dumezil, Georges. *Archaic Roman Religion* (vol. 1 & 2). Chicago: University of Chicago Press, 1996.

Editors of Time Life Books. *The Enchanted World: Fairies and Elves.* Chicago: Time Life Books, 1984.

Evans-Wentz, W. Y. *The Fairy Faith in Celtic Countries.* New York: Citadel Press, 1994.

Friend, Hilderick. *Flower Lore.* Rockport: Para Research, Inc., 1981.

Grieve, Mrs. M. *A Modern Herbal.* New York: Dover Publications, 1971.

Hazlitt, W. C. *Dictionary of Faiths & Folklore.* London: Bracken Books, 1995.

Hole, Christina. *A Dictionary of British Folk Customs.* Oxford: Helicon Publishing Ltd., 1995.

Jones, Alison. *Dictionary of World Folklore.* New York: Larousse, 1996.

Kerenyi, Carl. *Dionysos: Archetype Image of Indestructible Life.* Princeton: Princeton University Press, 1976.

Leland, Charles. *Etruscan Roman Remains.* London: T. Fischer Unwin, 1892.

Long, George. *The Folklore Calendar.* London: Random House UK, Ltd., 1996.

MacKillop, James. *Dictionary of Celtic Mythology.* Oxford: Oxford University Press, 1998.

Paterson, Jacqueline M. *Tree Wisdom: The Definitive Guidebook to the Myth, Folklore and Healing Power of Trees.* London: Thorsons, 1996.

Pepper, Elizabeth. *Celtic Tree Magic.* Middletown: The Witches' Almanac, Ltd., 1996.

Rankin, David. *Celts and the Classical World.* London: Routledge, 1996.

Saint, Christopher. *Insight into the Ancient Mysteries*. New York: Rivercross Publishing, Inc., 1997.

Scullard, H. H. *Roman Britain: Outpost of the Empire*. London: Thames and Hudson Ltd., 1979.

Turcan, Robert. *The Cults of the Roman Empire*. Oxford: Blackwell Publishers Ltd., 1996.

Vickery, Roy. *Oxford Dictionary of Plant-Lore*. New York: Oxford University Press, 1995.

INDEX

☾ REACH FOR THE MOON

Llewellyn publishes hundreds of books on your favorite subjects! To get these exciting books, including the ones on the following pages, check your local bookstore or order them directly from Llewellyn.

ORDER BY PHONE

- Call toll-free within the U.S. and Canada, 1-800-THE MOON
- In Minnesota, call (651) 291-1970
- We accept VISA, MasterCard, and American Express

ORDER BY MAIL

- Send the full price of your order (MN residents add 7% sales tax) in U.S. funds, plus postage & handling to:

  Llewellyn Worldwide
  P.O. Box 64383, Dept. 1-56718-283-6
  St. Paul, MN 55164–0383, U.S.A.

POSTAGE & HANDLING

(For the U.S., Canada, and Mexico)

- $4.00 for orders $15.00 and under
- $5.00 for orders over $15.00
- No charge for orders over $100.00

We ship UPS in the continental United States. We ship standard mail to P.O. boxes. Orders shipped to Alaska, Hawaii, The Virgin Islands, and Puerto Rico are sent first-class mail. Orders shipped to Canada and Mexico are sent surface mail.

International orders: Airmail—add freight equal to price of each book to the total price of order, plus $5.00 for each non-book item (audio tapes, etc.).

Surface mail—Add $1.00 per item.

Allow 2 weeks for delivery on all orders.
Postage and handling rates subject to change.

DISCOUNTS

We offer a 20% discount to group leaders or agents. You must order a minimum of 5 copies of the same book to get our special quantity price.

FREE CATALOG

Get a free copy of our color catalog, *New Worlds of Mind and Spirit*. Subscribe for just $10.00 in the United States and Canada ($30.00 overseas, airmail). Many bookstores carry *New Worlds*—ask for it!

Visit our website at www.llewellyn.com for more information.

HALLOWEEN
Customs, Recipes & Spells
Silver RavenWolf

Grab your flowing cape and journey through the history and magickal practices of America's favorite scary holiday. From Old World roots to New World charm, you will traverse the hodgepodge of legends and customs that created our modern tradition. *Halloween* brings you serious facts based on accurate research, as well as practical, how-to goodies and gossipy tidbits. Learn how history created many inaccurate myths about the original Halloween, which the ancient Celts called "Samhain," and how modern pagans still view it as a religious celebration. Discover practices, rituals, and recipes that honor the spirit of the holiday, which you can adapt to fit any spiritual orientation.

1-56718-719-6, 264 pp., 7½ x 9⅛, illus.   **$12.95**

YULE
A Celebration of Light & Warmth

Dorothy Morrison

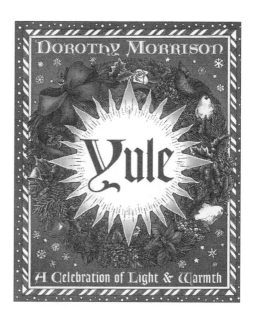

The "holidays": some call them Christmas or Hanukkah, others know them as Los Posadas or Ta Dhiu. Still others celebrate Winter Solstice or Yule. They are a time for reflection, resolution, and renewal. Whatever our beliefs, the holidays provide us with rituals to celebrate the balance of light and dark, and for welcoming the healing powers of warmth back into our world.

Jam-packed with more than sixty spells, invocations, and rituals, *Yule* guides you through the magic of the season. Traveling its realm will bring back the joy you felt as a child—the spirit of warmth and good will that lit the long winter nights. Discover the origin of the eight tiny reindeer, brew up some Yuletide coffee, and learn ways to create your own holiday traditions and crafts based on celebrations from a variety of countries and beliefs.

1-56718-496-0, 7½ x 9⅛, 216 pp., 56 illus. $17.95

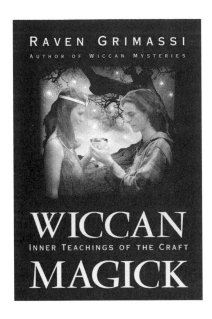

WICCAN MAGICK
Inner Teachings of the Craft

Raven Grimassi

Wiccan Magick is a serious and complete study for those who desire to understand the inner meanings, techniques, and symbolism of magick as an occult art. Magick within modern Wicca is an eclectic blending of many occult traditions that evolved from the ancient beliefs and practices in both Europe, the Middle East, and Asia. *Wiccan Magick* covers the full range of magickal and ritual practices as they pertain to both modern ceremonial and shamanic Wicca.

Come to understand the evolution of the Craft, the ancient magickal current that flows from the past to the present, and the various aspects included in ritual, spell casting, and general theology. When you understand why something exists within a ritual structure, you will know better how to build upon the underlying concepts to create ritual that is meaningful to you.

1-56718-255-0, 240 pp., 6 x 9 $12.95

TO ORDER, CALL 1-800 THE MOON
Prices subject to change without notice

THE WICCAN MYSTERIES
Ancient Origins & Teachings

Raven Grimassi

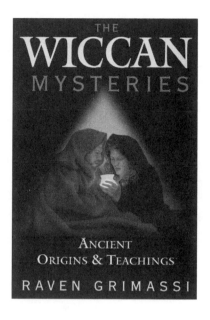

What you will encounter in *The Wiccan Mysteries* is material that was once taught only in the initiate levels of the old Wiccan Mystery Traditions, and to which many solitary practitioners have never had access. Learn the inner meanings of Wiccan rites, beliefs, and practices, and discover the time-proven concepts that created, maintained, and carried Wiccan beliefs up into this modern era. In reflecting back upon the wisdom of our ancestors, neo-Wiccans can draw even greater sustenance from the spiritual stores of Wicca—the Old Religion.

The Wiccan Mysteries will challenge you to expand your understanding and even reexamine your own perceptions. Wicca is essentially a Celtic-oriented religion, but its Mystery Tradition is derived from several outside cultures as well. You will come away with a sense of the rich heritage that was passed from one human community to another, and that now resides within this system for spiritual development.

1-56718-254-2, 312 pp., 6 x 9   **$14.95**

TO ORDER, CALL 1-800 THE MOON
Prices subject to change without notice

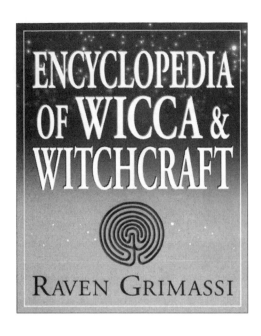

ENCYCLOPEDIA OF WICCA & WITCHCRAFT

Raven Grimassi

This indispensable reference work provides both a historical and cultural foundation for modern Wicca and Witchcraft, and it is the first to be written by an actual practitioner of the Craft.

Other encyclopedias present a series of surface topics such as tools, sabbats, Witchcraft trials, and various mundane elements. Unique to this encyclopedia is its presentation of Wicca/Witchcraft as a spiritual path, connecting religious concepts and spirituality to a historical background and a modern system of practice. It includes only Wicca/Witchcraft topics, old and new, traditional and eclectic, avoiding the inclusion of peripheral entries. It also features modern Wiccan expressions, sayings, and terminology. Finally, you will find a storehouse of information on European folklore and Western Occultism as related to modern Wicca/Witchcraft.

1-56718-257-7, 496 pp., 8 x 10, 300+ illus. & photos $24.95

TO ORDER, CALL 1-800 THE MOON
Prices subject to change without notice

HEREDITARY WITCHCRAFT
Secrets of the Old Religion

Raven Grimassi

This book is about the Old Religion of Italy, and contains material that is at least 100 years old, much of which has never before been seen in print. This overview of the history and lore of the Hereditary Craft will show you how the Italian witches viewed nature, magick, and the occult forces. Nothing in this book is mixed with, or drawn from, any other Wiccan traditions.

The Italian witches would gather beneath the full moon to worship a goddess (Diana) and a god (Dianus). The roots of Italian Witchcraft extend back into the prehistory of Italy, in the indigenous Mediterranean/Aegean neolithic cult of the Great Goddess. Follow its development to the time of the Inquisition, when it had to go into hiding to survive, and to the present day. Uncover surprising discoveries of how expressions of Italian Witchcraft have been taught and used in this century.

1-56718-256-9, 288 pp., 7½ x 9⅛, 31 illus.   **$14.95**

TO ORDER, CALL 1-800 THE MOON
Prices subject to change without notice

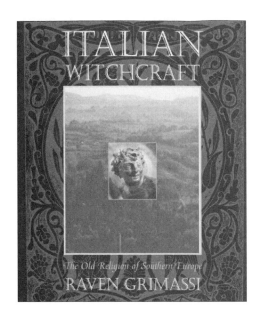

ITALIAN WITCHCRAFT
The Old Religion of Southern Europe

Raven Grimassi

(Formerly titled
Ways of the Strega,
now revised and expanded)

Discover the rich legacy of magick and ritual handed down by Italian witches through the generations. Trace the roots of the Italian Pagan tradition as it survives the times, confronted by Christianity, revived in the 14th century by the Holy Strega, and passed on as the Legend of Aradia to the present day. Explore the secrets of Janarra (lunar) witches, Tanarra (star) witches, and Fanarra (ley lines) witches. Their ancient wisdoms come together in the modern Aridian tradition, presented here for both theoretical understanding and everyday practice.

You will learn the gospel of Aradia, and the powerful practice of "casting shadows," an ancient tradition only now available to the public. *Italian Witchcraft* also gives you the practical how-tos of modern Strega traditions, including making tools, casting and breaking spells, seasonal and community rites, honoring the Watchers, creating a Spirit Flame, and much more.

1-56718-259-3, 336 pp., 7½ x 9⅛, illus.   **$14.95**

TO ORDER, CALL 1-800 THE MOON
Prices subject to change without notice

GREEN WITCHCRAFT
Folk Magic, Fairy Lore & Herb Craft

Aoumiel (Ann) Moura

Very little has been written about traditional family practices of the Old Religion simply because such information has not been offered for popular consumption. If you have no contacts with these traditions, *Green Witchcraft* will meet your need for a practice based in family and natural Witchcraft traditions.

Green Witchcraft describes the worship of nature and the use of herbs that have been part of human culture from the earliest times. It relates to the Lord and Lady of Greenwood, the Primal Father and Mother, and to the Earth Spirits called Faeries.

Green Witchcraft traces the historic and folk background of this path and teaches its practical techniques. Learn the basics of Witchcraft from a third-generation, traditional family Green Witch who openly shares from her own experiences. Through a how-to format you'll learn rites of passage, activities for Sabbats and Esbats, Fairy lore, self-dedication, self-initiation, spellwork, herbcraft, and divination.

This practical handbook is an invitation to explore, identify and adapt the Green elements of Witchcraft that work for you, today.

1-56718-690-4, 288 pp., 6 x 9, illus.   **$14.95**

TO ORDER, CALL 1-800 THE MOON
Prices subject to change without notice

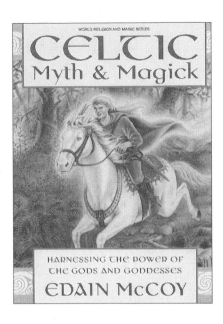

CELTIC MYTH & MAGIC
Harnessing the Power of the Gods & Goddesses

Edain McCoy

Tap into the mythic power of the Celtic goddesses, gods, heroes, and heroines to aid your spiritual quests and magickal goals. *Celtic Myth & Magic* explains how to use creative ritual and pathworking to align yourself with the energy of these archetypes, whose potent images live deep within your psyche.

Celtic Myth & Magic begins with an overview of forty-nine different types of Celtic Paganism followed today, then gives specific instructions for evoking and invoking the energy of the Celtic pantheon to channel it toward magickal and spiritual goals and into esbat, sabbat, and life transition rituals. Three detailed pathworking texts will take you on an inner journey where you'll join forces with the archetypal images of Cuchulain, Queen Maeve, and Merlin the Magician to bring their energies directly into your life. The last half of the book clearly details the energies of over 300 Celtic deities and mythic figures so you can evoke or invoke the appropriate deity to attain a specific goal.

This inspiring, well-researched book will help solitary Pagans who seek to expand the boundaries of their practice to form working partnerships with the divine.

1-56718-661-0, 464 pp., 7 x 10 $19.95

TO ORDER, CALL 1-800 THE MOON
Prices subject to change without notice